Collision Course:

The Ram And The Goat Of Daniel 8

JAMES F. MATHENY

And

MARJORIE B. MATHENY

Unless otherwise indicated, Scripture quotations are from the Authorized (King James) Version.

ISBN 0-939422-05-0

Edited by Debra Esolen

Cover by David Ned House

Jay & Associates, Publishers

P.O. Box 2222

Brevard, North Carolina 28712-2222

1993

Printed in the United States of America

CONTENTS

No student of the Scriptures should be satisfied to traffic only in the results of the study of other men. The field is inexhaustible and its treasures ever new. No worthy astronomer limits his attention to the findings of other men, but is himself ever gazing into the heavens both to verify and to discover; and no worthy theologian will be satisfied alone with the result of the research of other theologians, but will himself be ever searching the Scriptures.

Dr. Lewis Sperry Chafer

Preface

Before beginning our discussion of Daniel 8, we must explain two principles which are very important to the interpretation of the Bible, especially those passages dealing with prophecy: the first principle is that the Bible is its own best interpreter. Teaching derived from any particular passage must be fully supported elsewhere in the Bible. Unfortunately, Bible scholars have often resorted to current events or secular history to interpret the Word of God, a practice which has produced serious interpretive errors. In time these errors become entrenched, and few scholars attempt to dislodge established positions. Any means by which Satan can promote the reliance of students of the Word on some authority other than the Bible is clearly to his profit, since only the Bible can claim an infallible authority. If sources other than the Scriptures keep believers either unconcerned about or blinded to his approaching end or, better still, prejudiced against the idea of the certain and speedy overthrow of this active enemy of God and man, Satan clearly stands to gain. Speculation and subjective reasoning derived from extrabiblical sources, therefore, should have no value whatever in determining the ultimate truth of a biblical passage.

The second principle necessary to a proper understanding of the Bible, is not to stray from what Scripture actually says. This may sound elementary, but very often Scripture is misunderstood because it has not been read correctly *in its context*. And, since many difficulties arise as a result of translating from one language to another, it is best whenever possible to check readings in the original languages. It is especially incumbent on those who translate or teach to be faithful students of the original texts.

Recently we overheard a statement to the effect that all that could be written or said in interpreting the Bible has already been done. Such an attitude only discourages students from examining the wealth of biblical truth that has been ignored. Indeed, much remains to be discovered in the Scriptures. In his epistle to those in Rome, the Apostle Paul paid tribute to the limitlessness of our God and his Word:

> Romans 11:33 O the depth of the riches both of the wisdom and knowledge of God! how unsearchable are his judgments, and his ways past finding out!

A presumed derivative of "exereunao" meaning "to explore," or "search diligently,"[1] the Greek word here translated "unsearchable" should properly read "not searched out," Paraphrased the line would read, "how *unexplored* are his judgments," with the negative prefix indicating that the judgments of God have *not* been diligently "explored" or "searched out." The phrase which follows, "And his ways past finding out," should read "and his ways not tracked out". God's ways are *not* "past finding out," for the believer is admonished to have the mind of Christ (Philippians 2:5), but few there are who diligently follow the "track" of his ways. Spiritual growth is based on knowledge of God and His "ways," and the person who is not growing in knowledge is not growing spiritually. Like Paul, Peter admonished all Christians to cultivate this area:

> II Peter 3:18 But grow in grace, and in the knowledge of our Lord and Saviour Jesus Christ.

Were we to search the Scriptures every day for a thousand years we would only scratch the surface of the wealth it holds for mankind. Our Lord challenged Israel to search the Scriptures to prove or disprove His claims for He knew that only in those Scriptures would they find a record of absolute truth.

The 8th chapter of Daniel is one neglected portion of Scripture which cries out for clarification. It has not heretofore been sufficiently "tracked out." All of us are subject to mistakes. None but God has the last word on truth, but is it not better to risk a mistake in an honest effort to interpret a difficult passage rather than complacently continue teaching what we believe to be wrong? With these thoughts in mind, we present an interpretation which we believe is closer to the original intent of this long neglected chapter than that of the traditional view.

James F. Matheny
Marjorie B. Matheny

Chapter 1

Introduction

Relatively little *original study* on the text of Daniel has been conducted since the time of Jerome (347-420 A.D.), whose commentary on Daniel became the authority in his day and has remained so ever since. While a few evangelicals have written on the book, their basic outline adopts Jerome's interpretation. Wilbur Smith's statement is typical of this position:

> The most important single work produced by the Church Fathers on any of the prophetic writings of the Old Testament, commenting upon the original Hebrew text, and showing a complete mastery of all the literature of the Church on the subjects touched upon to the time of composition, is *without question* St. Jerome's Commentary on the Book of Daniel.[2]

There is no question but that Jerome's work became the single most important commentary ever written on the book of Daniel. From the vantage point of over 1500 years, however, we perceive some difficulties in evaluating the sources from which Jerome derived his conclusions. For example, Jerome borrowed much of his interpretation from Porphyry (233-305 A.D.), a third century A.D. pagan philosopher who, in attempting to discredit the book as a forgery, contended that the kingdoms of Daniel 2 were Babylon, Medo-Persia, Greece, and four kingdoms into which Alexander the Great's empire was divided after his death.

Adopting many of Porphyry's arguments for his identification of the kingdoms in Daniel 2, Jerome treated chapters 8-12 of Daniel as having been partially fulfilled during the intertestamental period but awaiting complete fulfillment in the end time. Jerome's own words in his commentary on Daniel attest to his conviction that the events of the intertestamental years partly fulfilled Daniel's prophecy (emphasis ours):

> Porphyry wrote his twelfth book against the prophecy of Daniel, (A) denying that it was composed by the person to whom it is ascribed in its title, but rather by some individual living in Judea at the time of Antiochus who was surnamed Epiphanes. He furthermore alleged that Daniel did not foretell the future so much as he related the past, and lastly, that whatever he spoke of up till the time of Antiochus contained authentic history, whereas anything he may have conjectured beyond that point was false, inasmuch as he would not have foreknown the future...And because Porphyry saw that *all these things had been fulfilled and could not deny that they had taken place, he overcame this evidence of historical accuracy by taking refuge in this evasion,* contending that whatever is foretold concerning Antichrist at the end of the world was actually fulfilled in the reign of Antiochus Epiphanes, because of certain similarities to things which took place at his time. *But this very attack testifies to Daniel's accuracy. For so striking was the reliability of what the prophet foretold, that he could not appear to unbelievers as a predictor of the future, but rather a narrator of things already past.*[3]

When Jerome accepted Porphyry's account of history following the death of Alexander the Great as the fulfillment of prophecy, he went astray; and modern interpreters who accept Jerome's conclusions fall into the same error.

Among   conservative   Christians   Jerome's

interpretation has become sacrosanct. With only some minor additions and alterations, Jerome's basic outline of prophecy has remained in place to our day.

With Julian the Apostate, the Emperor of Rome, however, having recently attempted to rebuild a temple in Jerusalem, Jerome believed that he must be living in the last days and accordingly altered Porphyry's original thesis to identify Rome as the final kingdom of Daniel's vision. Jerome, therefore, saw the four world empires of Daniel 2 as Babylon, Medo-Persia, Greece, and Rome; and Jerome was the one who originally proposed that Daniel 2 and Daniel 7 dealt with the same four kingdoms. The interpretation, moreover, which he based upon Julian's failed attempt to rebuild the Temple--Rome as the final kingdom of Daniel 2--ironically has remained the standard.

More recent commentators, concluding that Jerome's scenario had to be modified because Rome as an empire no longer exists, have espoused a "revival" of the Roman Empire. This position has again been established as tradition, but now the "little horn" of Daniel 7 is identified as a Roman ruler (the Antichrist) of the last days, whereas the "little horn" of Daniel 8 continues to be regarded as Antiochus Epiphanes of the intertestamental years. The four beasts out of the sea on which *the four winds of heaven* strive in Daniel 7 are said to symbolize the same kingdoms as do the gold, silver, brass, and iron in the image Nebuchadnezzar saw in his vision in chapter 2, while the "four notable ones" that come up toward *these same four winds of heaven* in chapter 8 are relegated to four "Greek" kingdoms that came into being after the death of Alexander the Great. Few seem to be bothered by the inconsistencies in this long-accepted interpretation.

The idea that Daniel 8 would be fulfilled in two stages, partly during the time of Antiochus Epiphanes and partly in the future, was handed down to the

10

Church by Jerome, who as we have already noted, borrowed his analysis from the neo-platonist philosopher, Porphyry. According to this traditional interpretation, there arose out of the former Greek empire a leader, Antiochus Epiphanes (the eigthth king in Syria) who reigned 174-163 B.C. He invaded Palestine, persecuted the Jews, and allowed one of his generals to slaughter a pig upon the altar, thus desecrating the Temple.[1] Traditionalists state that chapter 8 not only deals with Antiochus Epiphanes but that it forshadows the end time when another desolator will come to Israel and again desecrate the Holy Place. Talbot's evaluation of the text is typical of this view (emphasis ours):

> When the vision recorded here was given to Daniel, all of it had to do with then prophetic events; whereas we today can look back and see that everything in verses 1-22 refers to men and empires that have come and gone. *We read about them in the pages of secular history.* But verses 23-27 of the chapter before us have to do with "a king of fierce countenance" who shall appear in the latter time (verse 23); and he is none other than the Antichrist who is to come. Again, while verses 1-22 have to do with history, yet the men of whom they speak were shadows of that coming "man of sin," who is more fully described in the closing verses of the chapter.[4]

While subscribing to this dual fulfillment of Daniel's prophecy by Antiochus and a final Roman ruler, Scofield added to the scholarly confusion by

---

[1] Too often Bible scholars credit Antiochus Epiphanes with desecrating the Temple but it was Apollonius, the leading general of Antiochus, who actually sacrificed on the altar.

distinguishing the "little horn" of Daniel 7 from the "little horn" of Daniel 8 even though Daniel himself had been careful to link the two visions together (Daniel 8:26). The following is drawn from Scofield's notes:

> (8:9) The "little horn" of this verse (cp. v. 23) was fulfilled (171-164 B.C.) in the historical Antiochus Epiphanes, who came out of Syria (one of the four notable kingdoms of vv. 8, 22), and persecuted the Jews and profaned the Temple at Jerusalem. He is not to be confused with the "little horn" of 7:8, who is yet to come in the tribulation period (see vv. 9-13, 23). The "little horn" of 7:8 will rise from the ten horns into which the fourth empire (Roman) will be divided, whereas the "little horn" of Ch. 8 comes out of one of the four horns (vv. 9,22) into which the third empire (Grecian) is divided after Alexander's death (vv. 21-22) in the latter time of the four kingdoms of Alexander's generals (v. 23). Both "little horns" are violent in their hatred of the Jews and of God, and in their profaning of the Temple at Jerusalem (cp. 7:25 and 8:10-12).[5]

As Walvoord explains (emphasis ours):

> It may be concluded that many premillennial expositors find a *dual fulfillment* in Daniel 8: some of them achieve this by a division of the first part of the chapter as historically fulfilled and the last part prophetically future, some regard the whole chapter as having, in some sense, a *dual fulfillment* historically as well as in the future; but most of them find the futuristic elements emphasized in the interpretation of the vision.[6]

The idea of a dual fulfillment of Daniel 8 (and its almost universal acceptance among premillennial conservatives) needs to be challenged. Subjectively dividing this chapter into events of both the intertestamental period and the end time must be carefully examined. Interpreters do not agree on several points, and, obviously, not all of these views can be correct.

We can present four observations which cast doubt upon any theory of dual fulfillment: 1) as we noted in our preface, secular history and non-canonical literature, which provide the foundational underpinning of the speculative reasoning behind this idea, should not form the basis for Bible interpretation, 2) as we also noted in our preface, Scripture is its own best interpreter, 3) Daniel 8:17 and 19 specifically state that the "vision" applies to the time of the end, and the intertestamental period was not the time of the end, 4) God does not rely on pagans such as Porphyry to interpret His Word for His people. This is inadmissable.

We would like to simplify the text on this point by asserting that the "little horn" of Daniel 7:8 is the same "little horn" in Daniel 8:9.[2] To believe otherwise is to ignore Gabriel's specific statement that the entire book of Daniel deals with the end time (Daniel 12:4,9). Since Gabriel specifically assigned Daniel 8:1-14 to the end time period (8:17, 19) and since the end of time has not yet come, all the events described therein must yet be future. Neither Jerome, nor certainly Porphyry, had the power to break the seal noted in the following (emphasis ours):

Daniel 12:4 But thou, O Daniel, *shut up the words, and seal the book, even to the time of the end*...(Daniel 8:17, 19, 26; 12:9).

---

[2] See our study on The Four Beasts of Daniel 7. We add to that explanation later in this book.

Only as the end of time approaches will the seal be broken and the contents of Daniel understood. We agree with most conservatives who believe that we are now living in the last days. In that case, we can expect the seal which kept former generations from understanding Daniel to be removed and further study in this area to prove especially fruitful. Since Jerome's interpretation of Daniel has until now been the standard, the only prophetic view put forth by conservatives, a new study of the text is warranted.

Tradition, Good And Bad

Tradition can be at times both good and bad, depending on the circumstances. The Scriptures teach us to preserve the old landmarks, that is, certain traditions:

Proverbs 22:28 Remove not the ancient landmark, which thy fathers have set.

Certain customs of the culture of our ancestors remind us of our origins and distinguish our roots. As Isaiah instructed the children of Israel:

Isaiah 51:1 Hearken to me, ye that follow after righteousness, ye that seek the Lord: look unto the rock whence ye are hewn, and to the hole of the pit whence ye are digged.

2 Look unto Abraham your father, and unto Sarah that bare you: for I called him alone, and blessed him, and increased him.

Israel was encouraged to embrace the truth which was handed down from the father and mother of their nation. While some would do away with many of the traditions of our ancestors, there are traditions which should be retained. Job rebuked Eliphaz for being too hasty in that regard, as we see in the following:

> Job 24:1 Why, seeing times are not hidden from the Almighty, do they that know him not see his days?
>
> 2 Some remove the landmarks; they violently take away flocks, and feed thereof.

Scripture teaches us, then, to avoid breaking with tradition without considerable thought. Conversely, however, Scripture also warns us of times when observing men's traditions has been detrimental. It can be a barrier to the effectual working of the Word of God as we see in our Lord's rebuke of Pharisaic Judaism:

> Matthew 15:1 Then came to Jesus scribes and Pharisees, which were of Jerusalem, saying,
>
> 2 Why do thy disciples transgress the traditions of the elders? for they wash not their hands when they eat bread.
>
> 3 But he answered and said unto them, Why do ye also transgress the commandment of God by your tradition?
>
> 6 ...Thus have ye made the commandment of God of none effect by your tradition.
>
> 9 ...But in vain they do worship me, teaching for doctrines the commandments of men.

By substituting the teachings of men, which became

traditional, for the commandments of God, Israel rendered the Word of God of no effect. Unfortunately, Christianity has adopted some of the same practices.

We must not blindly follow traditional interpretations when plainly those teachings do not stand up under the scrutiny of the Word. Unless we find it substantiated in later revelation, dual fulfillment can only be an accommodation to error. This kind of tradition bears investigation. The following points briefly underscore components of the traditional interpretation which need to be reexamined in light of the text itself:

The Ram As Ancient Media And Persia

Because "the two horns were high; but one was higher than the other, and the higher came up last" (Daniel 8:3), the Ram is traditionally identified as the ancient Medo-Persian Empire. Since Persia eventually subjugated Media, conservative reasoning finds ancient Media represented by the short horn and Persia represented by the horn that was higher and came up last. The trouble with this idea is that Persia, under Cyrus, was already in control of the entire Empire when the Medo-Persian Empire entered divine revelation. History gives the following account of the rise of the Medo-Persian Empire--which conquered territory to the west and south as well as to the east (emphasis ours):

> During the long reign of Nebuchadnezzar, the Chaldean empire flourished; but after his death Chaldean power quickly crumbled. Meanwhile the Persians suddenly rose to prominence and soon eclipsed all the great states of the ancient world. Within twenty years Cyrus the Great, the vigorous Persian leader, created a great empire. In 550 B.C. he threw off the Median yoke and, after defeating King Croesus four years later, he gained control of the Lydian

kingdom and of those Greek cities in Asia Minor which were under the nominal control of Lydia. Then he turned east, establishing his power *as far as the frontier of India.*[78]

While the above is an accurate synopsis of the rise of the ancient Medo-Persian Empire, the kingdom described in Daniel 8:4 *does not* conquer in the east (emphasis ours).

> Daniel 8:4 I saw the ram pushing *westward, and northward, and southward;* so that no beasts might stand before him, neither was there any that could deliver out of his hand; but he did according to his will, and became great.

If we believe every word in Scripture is divinely appointed, someone erred in applying this passage to the Medo-Persian Empire of Daniel's day. A closer look in the following chapters of this book will identify the Ram with the Medo-Persian Empire of the last days which we call by its more recent title--Iran.

The Goat As Greece

According to both Porphyry and Jerome, the Goat of Daniel 8 symbolized Greece as the kingdom that ran on the Ram. This view has since been adopted by virtually all conservatives. Walvoord agrees with this analysis:

> Interpreters of Daniel 8 are generally agreed that the he goat or literally, "buck of goats," represents the king of Greece, and more particularly the single important horn between its eyes, as also stated in Daniel 8:21, is "the first king," that is, Alexander the Great. All the facts about this goat and his activities obviously anticipate the dynamic role of Alexander.[9]

Here we must insist, as graciously but as firmly as we can, that nothing in Scripture "obviously anticipates" any role to be played by Alexander the Great. His activities took place during the intertestamental period, when God was silent to the nation and Israel was under ever increasing discipline from God because of their apostasy (See Malachi 2:7-9). In our book, *Gold, Silver, Brass, Iron, Rethinking the Kingdoms of Daniel 2,* we challenged Jerome's identification of both the brass and the iron kingdoms. He saw the brass kingdom as Greece under the leadership of Alexander the Great and the iron kingdom as Rome. Several errors surround this evaluation of the role of Greece in Daniel's vision.

To begin, Greece never became a world kingdom. A Macedonian, Alexander was a maurading general whose ambition it was to conquer the world. That ambition, which lasted only 12 years during which he was constantly on the move, is recorded in secular history *alone*, as the following excerpt from *Civilization, Past and Present* illustrates:

> Reveling in the heroic deeds of the Iliad, Alexander resolved to spread Greek culture throughout the world. Two years after Philip's death, Alexander set out to conquer the East with an army of 35,000 soldiers recruited from Macedonia and the league. In quick succession he subdued Asia Minor, Syria, Palestine, and Egypt. Then he marched to the Fertile Crescent and, in 331 B.C., defeated the powerful forces of Darius III, the Persian monarch.[10]

Although Alexander planned a Western Mediterranean campaign, he never lived to carry it out. His lust to conquer was brought to a halt when he died in a drunken stupor in Babylon at the age of thirty three. He never lived to rule an empire as Nebuchadnezzar did over Babylon, Cyrus over the Medo-Persian Empire, or Augustus over Rome.

Moreover, Alexander lived during the intertestamental period, a time of darkness for Israel when no divine revelation was given. If the Bible is its own best interpreter, then the theories of Porphyry and Jerome must be ruled out, since neither Alexander nor Antiochus Epiphanes is mentioned in God's divine record.

Gabriel told Daniel, upon God's directive, just when the events of Daniel 8 would take place:

Daniel 8:16 ...Gabriel, make this man to understand the vision.

17 So he came near where I stood: and when he came, I was afraid, and fell upon my face: but he said unto me, Understand, O son of man: for *at the time of the end shall be the vision.*

To place the events of Daniel 8 in the intertestamental period when God was silent, or even to call for a dual fulfillment of the prophecy is inconsistent with what the Word says.

Much of the misinformation about the role of Greece in Daniel's vision stems from the interpreters' assumption that the Hebrew word they have chosen to translate "Grecia," or "Greece," in 8:21, 10:20, and 11:2 did, in fact, refer solely to the country of Greece. The word, however, is "Javan" (in secular history "Ionians") which refers to all those descended from the fourth son of Japheth (Genesis 10:2) who settled the entire northern and western coasts of the Mediterranean basin. They were the primary progenitors of our present Western world and certainly were not confined to the Greece of Alexander's day.

The Four Notable Ones As Alexander's Generals

Porphyry proposed that after the death of Alexander, his kingdom was divided into four parts represented by the "four notable ones" mentioned in Daniel 8:

> Daniel 8:8 Therefore the he goat waxed very great: and when he was strong, the great horn was broken; and for it came up four notable ones toward the four winds of heaven.

> 22 Now that being broken, whereas four stood up for it, four kingdoms shall stand up out of the nation, but not in his power.

This view has been adopted, not only by Jerome, but by virtually every other commentator of the conservative community without careful examination. Walvoord confirms this interpretation:

> Practically all commentators, however, recognize the four horns as symbolic of the four kingdoms of the Diadochi which emerged as follows: (1) Cassander assumed rule over Macedonia and Greece; (2) Lysimacus took control of Thrace, Bithynia, and most of Asia Minor; (3) Seleucus took Syria and the lands to the east including Babylonia; (4) Ptolemy established rule over Egypt and possibly Palestine and Arabia Petraea. A fifth contender for political power, Antigonus, was soon defeated. Thus, with remarkable accuracy, Daniel in his prophetic vision predicts that the empire of Alexander was divided into four divisions, not three or less or five or more.[11]

This opinion that the four notable ones "toward the four winds of heaven" were the kingdoms ruled by Alexander's four generals after his death, requires some reexamination.

Not only is Alexander never recorded in Scripture but even secular history does not support a four-part division of Alexander's empire as may be noted in the following (emphasis ours):

> Alexander's death destroyed his plans for the "marriage of Europe and Asia." Since he left no heirs of suitable age or sufficient ability to carry on his mission, a struggle for power among his generals ensued. *Within a few decades* the empire was roughly divided among the African, Asian, and European elements: Egypt was ruled by the Ptolemy family; Alexander's conquered lands in Asia were governed by Seleucus and his descendants; and Macedonia and Greece constituted a separate power under Antigonus Gonatas. This *three part division of Alexander's empire* constituted the Hellenistic world and lasted for three centuries--a period historians call the Hellenistic Age, dating from Alexander's death in 323 B.C. to the battle of Actium in 31 B.C.[12]

The reality of a three-part division of Alexander's "empire" instead of four also calls into question the accuracy of the traditional interpretation of chapter 8. Further, since a Greek "empire" as such never really existed, it is proper to seek another explanation of this prophecy.

Assigning the "four notable ones" to Alexander's generals places the fulfillment of God's prophecy outside the bounds of revelation. These were events of the intertestamental years, a period of no revelation to Israel and a time of divine discipline on the nation. It, in fact, relies solely on extrabiblical sources, not the Scriptures, for authentication of the interpretation.

Since the two visions of Daniel 7 and 8 are linked together in 8:26 as "the vision of the evening and the morning," the phrase "the four winds of heaven" characterizes, not only the "four notable ones" of Daniel 8:8 but the four beasts of 7:2-3. As demonstrated in the previous book of this series, *The Four Beasts Of Daniel 7*, whatever kingdoms these "four beasts" (in chapter 7) or "four notable ones" (in chapter 8) signify, they are world-wide in scope as denoted by "the four winds of heaven" which bring them into being striving on the whole "sea" of humanity. The kingdoms of Alexander's generals were not global.

Rome As The Iron Kingdom

Jerome contended that Rome was the iron kingdom, the fourth kingdom of the image in Daniel 2. Thus he also identified Rome as the kingdom of the "beast diverse from them all," in Daniel 7. The traditional view has adopted this position with a slight modification to accommodate the disintegration of the Roman Empire shortly after the time of Jerome. Rather than point out that he had obviously been wrong, those who followed Jerome's identification of the four kingdoms in Daniel 2 found a way to rationalize their position with a new theory--that Rome will be revived in the end time.

Our studies of the text in Daniel 2 indicated to us that Rome under Caesar Augustus, rather than the fourth and final kingdom was, in fact, the third world empire symbolized by brass. (For the details of this position please refer to the second book of this series, *Gold, Silver, Brass, Iron: Rethinking the Kingdoms of Daniel 2.*)

While we do not think it necessary to go to secular writings to prove the truth of the Bible, some may find comfort in the fact that even secular history supports Rome as the brass kingdom. Callie Williamson, Johns Hopkins University, wrote a paper relating the use of bronze (brass) in the Roman Empire. Her conclusions substantiate our thesis that brass symbolized Rome. Please note the following from her paper (emphasis ours):

> Throughout the Republic and Empire (roughly
> from the fifth century B.C. to the sixth century
> A.D.) the Romans regularly had statutes,
> decrees, treaties, and edicts engraved on
> bronze tablets. Some statutes and interstate
> treaties were engraved exclusively on bronze,
> never on stone. Bronze tablets survive only
> from the second century B.C. onward, but
> ancient writers testify that bronze tablets had
> been engraved with statutes and treaties in
> Rome before the beginning of the Republic.
> And the practice persisted until A.D. 500.[13]

The extent of the use of bronze to record and preserve
the statutes, treaties and laws of Rome lasted over
1000 years. The author goes on to say:

> The conventional wisdom is that bronze tablets
> cumulatively constituted an official archive,
> which the Roman elite used in planning
> subsequent legislation and policy, and to which
> Romans of all classes had access. In this view
> statutes, decrees, treaties, and edicts were
> engraved to provide Romans and others with
> permanent, official versions of those
> documents, always available for consulting,
> copying, reading. In sum, bronze tablets were
> useful and efficient.[14]

While the author argues that these bronze tablets were
most inconvenient, she does support their usage
(emphasis ours):

> So why did Romans engrave legal documents
> on bronze tablets? My answer to this question
> concentrates on their *symbolic, one could almost
> say religious, aspects. I shall argue that bronze
> tablets were monuments: long enduring, ceremonial
> displays of law.* Consider for a moment the

23

visual impact of the tablets on display in Rome's public spaces. The largest concentration by far was on the Capitoline hill, Rome's ritual center, site of the huge temple of Jupiter built by Catulus, dedicated in 69 B.C. and rebuilt several times on an even grander scale. In the first century A.D., at least three thousand bronze tablets of statutes, treaties, honorific decrees, and grants of citizenship and other privileges hung there...We can visualize three thousand bronze tablets, shining polished in the Roman sun. If anything, that number was an understatement.[15]

Williamson adds (emphasis ours):

The celebration, the ceremony, and the ritual surrounding the publication are striking confirmation that the tablets, set into stone pillars, were not seen merely as archival records. Instead, *they were symbols of Rome and of Roman presence*...In summary, the effects of engraving on bronze were complex and varied. But they unite all Roman legal documents into a single class of ancient evidence: *bronze tablets symbolized grandeloquent rule and the majesty of law.*[16]

While Williamson's conclusions are impressive, the identifying trademark from the Scriptures distinguishing Rome as the brass kingdom of the image of Daniel 2 appears in the fulfillment of Daniel's own description of the brass kingdom! He had pinpointed that kingdom as "another third kingdom of bronze, which shall bear rule over *all the earth*" (Daniel 2:39). The realization of that prophecy is found in Luke 2:1:

Luke 2:1 And it came to pass, in those days, that there went out a decree from Caesar Augustus, that *all the world* should be taxed.

Alexander's conquered territory never qualified as an empire which bore rule "over all the earth." At best, it provided the culture and language which eventually permeated the Roman State. This fact, along with many other textual proofs detailed in our second book, rules out Greece as the third kingdom. So where does this leave the student of Scripture? It should lead him to question Jerome's interpretation and *drive him back to the Scriptures alone for his answers.*

Outline Of Daniel 8

The book of Daniel is divided into three parts. Daniel 1:1-2:3 (written in Hebrew) gives a brief history of Daniel and three of his Hebrew friends as young men captured by the armies of Nebuchadnezzar and deported into servitude in Babylon. Their refusal to conform to the ways of the Chaldeans (by eating food offered to their idols) gained them a reputation which was used to the glory of God. Their faithfulness was a powerful testimony to the other Jewish captives as well as to the reigning monarchs of both the Babylonian and the later Medo-Persian Empires.

Daniel 1:17 As for these four children, God gave them knowledge and skill in all learning and wisdom: and Daniel had understanding in all visions and dreams.

20 And in all matters of wisdom and understanding, that the king inquired of them, he found them ten times better than all the magicians and astrologers that were in all his realm.

21 And Daniel continued even unto the first year of king Cyrus.

The second section, Daniel 2:4-7:28 (written in Aramaic), while an integral part of Israel's Scripture, emphasizes the fate of nations of the world other than Israel. The image in Daniel 2 was prophetic of the four great kingdoms, beginning with Babylon, that would dominate the world scene from Daniel's time until the end. Daniel 7 deals exclusively with the formation, out of all the nations, of the last great kingdom, the kingdom of the "little horn," commonly referred to as the "Antichrist." The use of the Aramaic, which was the trade and diplomatic language among the nations of that day, draws our attention to the fact that the content, not only of chapter 2 but of chapter 7 involves other nations, not Israel exclusively.

Daniel 8:1-12:13, the third division of the book, concerns the fate of *Israel* in the last days. Written once more in Hebrew, the language of God's people, this section offers another change in emphasis. No longer concerned with the nations in general, this portion of Daniel reflects a renewed focus on Israel. An important point must be made here: *if the text of chapter 8 had dealt principally with a Gentile nation (Greece is usually seen as the Goat while later in the text Rome is inferred by the commentators) Daniel would almost certainly have continued this account in Aramaic.* Moreover, these last chapters of Daniel, dealing as they do with Israel, account for Daniel's emotional reaction to the revelation he had received about the destiny of his own people (Daniel 8:27, 10:23,8,16).

Following the teachings of Porphyry and Jerome that we mentioned earlier, traditionalists contend that a large portion of chapter 8 alludes to history which took place during the intertestamental period. As we also noted, they see Medo-Persia symbolized by the Ram, Greece under Alexander the Great by the Goat, and a supposed four divisions of Alexander's empire after his death by "the four notable ones".

A record of Daniel's second vision, chapter 8 does not deal with the intertestamental era. Instead, if we are to believe the scriptural account of Gabriel's words to Daniel, chapter 8 reveals what will happen to Israel in the last days, as the world embraces the "little horn," the final world ruler. Daniel 7 and 8 are a revelatory couplet picturing what will occur in the last days, not only to the other nations of the world but to Israel as well. Gabriel himself revealed the two visions to be equal parts of one revelation:

> Daniel 8:26 And the vision of the evening and the morning which was told is true: wherefore shut thou up the vision; for it shall be for many days.

As Daniel notes in the first two verses of each chapter, the vision of chapter 7 occurred at night and that of chapter 8 in the day time. The combined visions outline the summation of man's rule apart from God-- both in Israel as well as in all other nations. Both visions are true and will certainly come to pass. However, Daniel is careful to note Gabriel's warning seen in the reference above that both are for the last days--"for it shall be for many days" (Daniel 8:26).

Daniel 8 complements the content of Daniel 7 by filling in many details of end-time events. While Daniel 7 identifies the four beasts out of the sea as four kingdoms encompassing all regions of the globe out of which will come the "little horn," chapter 8 reveals specific events which will lead to the formation of these *four kingdoms*. Briefly summarizing, the conflict in chapter 8 between the Ram, (Iran), and the Goat, (the nations of Javan), ends in mutual catastrophe. A vacuum created by the weakened condition of these great powers in the world gives rise to the four kingdoms called "the four notable ones." Indeed, the spiritual forces by which these events are brought to pass are identified in *both* chapters as "the four winds of heaven" (Daniel 7:2; Daniel 8:8). This identifying phrase ties the four kingdoms found in both chapters together. Chapter 8 then proceeds directly to a discussion of how this chain of events will affect Israel through the coming of the "little horn."

Had scholars not been confused by the interjection of intertestamental history, the steady progression of detail unveiling the end time from Daniel 7 through Daniel 12 would have been noted sooner. But even this erroneous interpretation served God's purpose to shut and seal the vision as He had directed (8:26). One of the great "apocalyptic" (meaning "revelation, revealing, unveiling or disclosing"), books of the Bible, Daniel may be understood only by a comparison of its symbols, signs, and sayings with other portions of Scripture which interpret those symbols, signs, and sayings. In apocalyptic literature, one cannot discover the truth of visions, symbols, and signs by one's own ingenuity or by reference to secular writings. The only accurate interpretor of the symbolism of Scripture is Scripture.

A Word About The Prophet Daniel

Daniel was a unique person whose devotion to God is evident throughout the entire book. In chapter 1, we read of his faithfulness to God in choosing his diet and of his reward for this stand. In chapter 2, we read of his supernatural interpretation of Nebuchadnezzar's dream, given when his life and the lives of his friends and the other Chaldean wise men hung in the balance. Chapter 4 continues an account of his spiritual service to Nebuchadnezzar. We read in chapter 5 that Belshazzar, the last king of Babylon, was forced to call upon Daniel once again as the only faithful source for interpreting the handwriting on the wall. We find in chapter 6 that Daniel, ever faithful in prayer, was preserved in the lion's den. In chapter 9, his prayer of intercession for Israel resulted in great honor when God sent Gabriel to instruct him. A man "greatly beloved" by God (9:23), Daniel was entrusted with the revelation outlined in the book; but with the completion of the message, he was admonished to close and seal the book until the time of the end. Neither Jerome, nor certainly the pagan Porphyry, could have given the correct interpretation of Daniel's vision until the appointed time of God's unveiling. Now is the time for students of the Word to consider the text of the book of Daniel anew. We are surely living in the last days of which the prophet wrote.

End Notes

1. Strong, page 29
2. Smith, page 5
3. Jerome, pages 15-16
4. Talbot, page 143
5. Scofield, page 910
6. Wallbank, Taylor, Bailkey, page 58
7. Ibid, page 58
8. Classical Antiquity, Vol. 6/April, 1987, page 168
9. Ibid, page 163
10. Ibid, page 165
11. Ibid, pages 182-183

THE MOSLEM WORLD ca. 1950

Moslems predominate

" " form large minorities

" (in Africa) present as
soldiers, traders, missionaries etc.

142   Total population of area,
in hundreds of thousands

129   Moslems in area,
in hundreds of thousands

PACIFIC OCEAN

INDIAN OCEAN

ATLANTIC OCEAN

CASPIAN SEA

RED SEA

MEDITERRANEAN SEA

BLACK SEA

PERSIAN G.

Emery Walker Ltd. sc.

Chapter 2

The Ram

Daniel 8:1   In the third year of the reign of king Belshazzar a vision appeared unto me, even unto me Daniel, after that which appeared unto me at the first.

Daniel 8 is divided into two parts. Verses 1-14 record Daniel's vision, and verses 15-27 provide the interpretation, explaining how the first 14 verses fit into the overall prophetic plan. According to verse 1, Daniel received this revelation in the third year of the reign of King Belshazzar (Daniel 8:1). If we may rely on the Babylonian Chronicle's chronology of the kings of Babylon, the vision of chapter 7 occurred in about 553 B.C., and the vision of chapter 8 occurred two years later (551 B.C.)--about 12 years before the overthrow of Belshazzar (539 B.C.) and the end of the Babylonian Empire (as recorded in Daniel 5). In addition to the dating of the vision, there are several other circumstances found in verses 1 and 2 that we will touch on briefly.

In the clause, "A vision appeared unto me" the word translated "vision" ("hazon") is an exalted term used to describe a special art of seeing, conveyed only to special people. As HAW explains:

The revelatory vision is granted by God to chosen messengers, i.e., prophets. Such apparently was the experience of Balaam, the son of Beor (Num 24:4,16). This vision of the prophets took place sometimes in the waking state, but also in "the spirit."[1]

Used in the passive sense "hazon" means to receive special knowledge of divine things. In Daniel's case, the prophet sometimes had to have the meaning of what he had received explained to him by a messenger from God.

The phrase "After that which appeared unto me at the *first*," refers to the "first vision," which Daniel had received two years previously (Daniel 7). The word translated "first" in this passage ("tehilla") is the same word used in Daniel 9:21 where it is translated "beginning." According to HAW:

> Tehilla, beginning, first (in a series). This feminine noun, derived from the Hiphil of "halal" discussed above is used twenty-two times in three categories. First, it marks the first of a series of occurrences, the outset, as of a journey (Gen 13:3; 41:21) or the first in order of attack (Jud 1:1). Secondly, the most commonly, it refers to the "beginning" of a specified time, e.g., the barley harvest (Ruth 1:22), the growth of vegetation (Amos 7:1), or the occupation of Samaria by Babylonian deportees (II Kgs 17:25). It is used of the first words of a prayer (Daniel 9:23) or of the first words of a godless man's speech (Eccl 10:13). Thirdly, in an abstract sense, it denotes the "first principle" of wisdom, which is the fear of the Lord (Prov 9:10).[2]

The vision recorded in Daniel 7 was the first given to Daniel personally; that recorded in chapter 8 is the second. Both passages deal exclusively with events of the last days, but whereas the first vision relates events of the last days as they affect all kingdoms of the world, the second deals primarily with events as they affect the nation of Israel. We will see later that part of Daniel 8 aids in the interpretation of Daniel 7 and vice versa. The usage of the word "first" as described in HAW's explanation above ties the two chapters together as a series on the same subject matter, in this case, the events of the end time.

In verse 2 of chapter 8, Daniel describes his location as Shushan (Susa in secular literature), one of the royal cities of Persia, located about 200 miles east of Babylon in the province of Elam. King Xerxes of Persia later built a palace at Shushan which was also the location of events in the book of Esther (Esther 1:2). Nehemiah became cup-bearer there to King Artaxerxes (Nehemiah 1:1). Although Daniel may have become familiar with the city of Shushan while serving in the court of Nebuchadnezzar, the fact that he saw himself there and was able to identify the palace is still significant, since in the time of Belshazzar when the vision was given the palace had not yet been built.

The city of Shushan (which in Hebrew means "rejoicing") was located in the province of Elam, named after the eldest son of Shem (Genesis 10:22). As Shem's eldest son, Elam should have received both the birthright and the blessing. While the Bible does not specify why that blessing was, in fact, passed to the third son, Arphaxad, we do know that Elam became a great kingdom known for its pagan worship. ISBE states:

The rediscovery of the history of Elam is one of

the most noteworthy things of modern research. It has revealed to us the wonderful development which that kingdom had made at an exceedingly early date, and shows that it was politically just as important as the Babylonian states 4,000 years BC, though probably hardly so advanced in art and lit.[3]

Daniel had, in fact, been transported to his Semitic beginnings in the vision to receive God's message of the end time.

The clause, "I was by the river of Ulai" is translated from a very difficult Hebrew construction which will require some detailed examination. Daniel's vision took place at the palace in Susa but the significance of the body of water is in doubt. We will focus our attention instead on some details in the language that draw our attention to God's purpose for setting Daniel's vision at a place whose very name connotes doubt or fear.

The passage begins with a personal pronoun which is then repeated, for emphasis, as part of the verb. Literally translated the passage reads, "I, I was" and lends special emphasis to the subject, Daniel. Following the verb we find the Hebrew word "al," a preposition which means "above, over, upon, or against" (translated here "by"). According to Brown, Driver, and Briggs this word "is used idiomatically to give pathos to the expression of an emotion, by emphasizing the person who is its subject, and who, as it were, feels it acting *upon* him."[4] Keeping that usage in mind, we see that the Hebrew word translated "river" is not the ordinary Hebrew expression for a river, but is derived from a prime root denoting the emotional response of"mourning, wailing, or lamenting." While the word following, "Ulai" has traditionally been translated as the name of the river, it can also be "expressing doubt, or fear." A literal rendering of this sentence should thus read: "I, I (emphasis *upon me*) was mournfully doubting" or paraphrased, "I, I was lamenting my fear."

Read literally, this passage describes Daniel obviously fearful of something he only partially understood. In a place of "rejoicing," Daniel was gripped by emotions that expressed just the opposite, perhaps because of apprehension engendered by his first vision just 2 years before. This sentence sets the tone for the rest of the vision where Daniel slowly grasped the truth concerning the end of history, a knowledge which sickened him (Daniel 8:27).

When we see the vision's effect on Daniel, we can better evaluate the effect it should have on us. Of all generations, we alone are living in the days when this prophecy is being fulfilled. The Scriptures are intended to prepare us for these events--mentally, emotionally, and most of all, spiritually. The activities of the kingdom symbolized by the Ram will signal the countdown to the final battle of Armageddon. Daniel 8 sets the stage for the events of the last days and shows us how swiftly the Lord will bring about the end once the nations are placed according to His design.

The Two Horned Ram

In verse 3 Daniel expands the scene of his second vision. One who is mourning usually has his head down, so not surprisingly Daniel says, "I lifted up my eyes." A common verb meaning "to see," the Hebrew word "raa" is of special importance when used as it is here, to describe the act of an authentic prophet receiving oracles from God. Then the word "hinneh," which follows, translated "behold" here, is an interjection demanding attention. It is used mainly to emphasize the information which follows: in this case Daniel was considering the appearance of a horned ram.

This sentence in the KJV reads, "behold, there stood before the river a ram" but literally translated reads, "Behold, one ram stood before the face of the mourner." The Hebrew word "echad" is present in this passage and should be translated "one." The text pointedly states that only one ram was present.

The emphasis on the fact that there is only one ram creates a problem. Verse 20 tells us that "The ram which thou sawest having two horns are the kings of Media and Persia." "Kings" (plural) has led some scholars to divide the kingdom into separate kingdoms of the Medes and the Persians, but to answer this problem we note that while the word "kings" is plural there remains but one ram and this Ram represents one undivided kingdom of the Medes and the Persians. Throughout history the Ram has been the symbol of the Medo-Persian Empire. According to Keil:

In the *Bundehesch* the guardian spirit of the Persian kingdom appears under the form of a ram with clean feet and sharp-pointed horns, and ...the Persian king, when he stood at the head of his army, bore, instead of a diadem, the head of a ram.[5]

35

Throughout the Bible, the "horn" denotes authority and power. Since the Ram represents the kings of Media and Persia, we suggest the short horn indicates authority in the past (Medo-Persia in the days of Daniel) and the higher horn indicates authority in the last days (latter day Medo-Persia, or Iran).

Again, as it was in the second verse, the word translated "river" should more accurately be rendered as a "mourner," one who laments, expressing his doubt and fear. Let us emphasize that the Ram was standing before Daniel who was mourning and in fear for his people, Israel.

The next phrase "which had horns" introduces the concept of the Ram's power. The common, figurative use of "horn" in the Old Testament is taken from the image of battling animals to denote aggressive strength. In Scripture to "exalt the horn" is to be clothed with strength (I Samuel 2:1-10). To "cut off the horn" is to rob of strength (Psalm 75:10; Jeremiah 48:25). Quoting L. Schmidt, HAW states:

> In the OT the horn is not only an expression for physical power in symbolical prophetic action (II Kgs 22:11) or in visionary depiction of the might which has scattered Israel (Zech 2:1-4); it is a direct term for power...Consequently, "horn" becomes a symbol for men endowed with such power (Dan 8:20-21).[6]

While the horns of the Ram symbolize his power, this power is quantified by the word "high" ("The horns were high"). The Hebrew word "gabah," translated "high" in this passage, appears with its derivatives ninety-four times in the OT. Its basic meaning, "high, lofty, or exalted," "gabah" describes the height of persons, objects, places, it denotes high mountains, high hills, the gates of Babylon, high towers, and even the high gallows on which Haman was hung (Esther 7:9-10).[7] Sometimes the word suggests pride or haughtiness. Used in this passage where horns signify the power and authority of the Ram, the word indicates that his authority and power were exalted, perhaps even that he was haughty.

Unequal Horns, Unequal Power

The prophet tells us that the horns of the Ram were not equal. Literally the text reads: "And the one was higher (loftier) from the other." Thus one of the horns symbolized a more exalted authority than the other. This horn was raised to a greater height, and we read, "the higher came up last." Thus, the one with the most authority will be the last one to come up. We suggest that the Medo-Persian kingdom of the last days will be more extensive and will make a greater impact on the world than it has at any other time in its history. (Since this kingdom will extend throughout the Moslem world, we include a map at the end of chapter 1 to depict its reach.)

The Hebrew word "aharot," translated "last" in this part of Daniel's vision, comes from a root word that means *tarry, delay, defer*. HAW provides this pertinent explanation of the word (emphasis ours):

> Aharot. After part, latter part, future. Used sixty one times, this word is also not as common as some other derivatives, *but has theological import*. As is clear from other derivatives, the general meaning of the root is

after, later, behind, following...There are two theological questions at issue. First, does "aharit hayyamim (the end of the days) *refer to the general future, or more specifically to the last days, the final segment of time?*..The expression "Aharit hayyamim" is used fourteen times (Gen 49:1; Num 24:14; Deut 4:30; 31:29; Isa 2:2 = Mic 4:1; Jer 23:20; 30:24; 48;48; 49;39; Ezk 38:16; Dan 2:28; [Aram] and 10:14; Hos 3:5). The KJV translates Gen. Isa and Mic references with "*last days*," except for Gen and Deut 31:29 where it has "days to come." The NASB uses *latter days* in Deut 4:30; *last days* in Isa, Mic and Hos, *the future*" in Dan 10:14 and *days to come* in the other passages...It is possible to use this phrase both for the eschaton and for the general future because obviously all eschatology is future, but not all future is eschatology. It does seem clear that Isa 2:22 (Mic 4:1ff) refers to the eschaton ("last days" KJV, NSB, NIV).[8]

This long quote is given to show that the "higher horn" represents a kingdom that will be present "after, later, behind, following, future," that is, "last." Since the original Medo-Persian Empire certainly did not occur in the last days, one must consider the prophetic implication of a strengthened Iran in our own day.

Some commentators would have us believe that the smaller horn represented the Medes and the "higher" horn represented the Persians of ancient times, but this division does not fit the empire set forth in Scripture. ISBE defines the biblical Medo-Persian Empire as follows (emphasis ours):

Biblical history of the Persian empire *begins* with Cyrus the Great. Phaortes, king of the Medes, is said to have first subjugated the Persians to that kingdom about 97 years before Cyrus (Herod. i.102) Cyrus himself headed his countrymen's revolt against Astyages, who advanced to attack Pasargadae (549 B.C.). His army mutinied and surrendered him to Cyrus, whom the Greeks held to be his grandson on the mother's side. Cyrus, becoming supreme ruler of both Medes and Persians, advanced to the conquest of Lydia.[9]

Biblically speaking, the Medo-Persian Empire was always considered one empire and is referred to as such in Scripture. After the revolt led by Cyrus (550-549 B.C.), the Medes lost all semblance of self-determination and were entirely integrated into the Persian empire. As accurately as we can determine, at the time of Daniel's vision in the third year of Belshazzar (551 B.C.), the Medes and Persians were already poised for consolidation. After conquering Lydia in Asia Minor, Cyrus turned east, establishing his power as far as the frontier of India. Returning west, Babylon was third on his list, and with little resistance the city capitulated to the Medes and Persians in June, 538 B.C.

The horns did not, as is commonly taught, mark a division of the kingdom between the Medes and the Persians with the Persians exalted last. Medo-Persia was already one empire when it entered biblical revelation. We suggest (based on the meaning of the word "aharit" and its usage in Semitic studies) that the Ram represents the Medo-Persian Empire in both its former and latter manifestations. The smaller horn represents its degree of exaltation in the past under Cyrus the Great, its founder. The higher horn represents the power and authority of the Medo-Persian Empire in the future. The language of the passage emphasizes the second horn: "But the one higher was the second, and the higher came up last." Daniel's vision is concerned with the role Medo-Persia (present day Iran) will play in the last days.

Iran's Military Expansion

Verse 4 of Daniel's second vision provides an account of latter-day Medo-Persian expansion: "I saw the ram pushing westward, and northward, and southward." The word translated "pushing" here comes from the Hebrew word "nagach," a prime root meaning "to butt" with the horns; fig., to war against: gore, push (down, ing).[10] The word's derivative "naggah" means "addicted to goring" (Exodus 21:29, 36). The Ram's conquering will be accomplished through bloody warfare; but in contrast to Cyrus'campaigns, which pushed first westward to Asia Minor, then far to the east to India, and back again westward to conquer Babylon, the Ram of Daniel 8 will push westward, then northward, and finally southward. No mention is made of his pushing east.

Westward - Iraq, Jordan, Syria, Lebanon, and Turkey.

Northward - Armenian and Scythian nations (southern provinces of the former Soviet Union). Afghanistan, Pakistan and western China near Kashgar may be absorbed into the same sphere of influence apart from conquest. All of these areas are of the Moslem faith.

Southward - The Arabian peninsula, Gulf states, Ethiopia, and Egypt. Other Moslem countries such as Libya, the Sudan, Algeria, and Morocco may seek to join the same sphere of influence.

We should remember that sixty million Moslem people live in the former Soviet Union. Wherever Islam is predominent, present governments could conceivably be replaced by fundamentalist Islamic theocracies, by force if necessary. The Ram's expansion will be as the goring of a bull--painful and bloody and could obviously present a threat to Israel; but, as in the days of Abraham, the Ram will be sacrificed to protect the posterity of Abraham (Genesis 22:13).

In the next phrase, "No beasts might stand before him," "beast" is translated from the Hebrew word "chayuwth" meaning "life, living." The idea to be conveyed here is that nothing living will be able to stand before the awesome forces of the Ram.

The phrase, "neither was there any that could deliver out of his hand," should literally read, "And there was not delivered from his hand." The word "not" comes from the Hebrew word "ayin," whose prime root means "to be nothing or not exist, a non-entity."[11] No nation that the Ram wishes to conquer can be liberated from his hands. The word "deliver" in this passage is translated from the Hebrew word "natsal," a prime root meaning "to snatch away," whether in a good or bad sense; it corresponds to a Chaldean word meaning "to extricate: deliver, rescue." At the time of his conquests, no power sufficient to rescue those in the path of the Ram's power and cruelty will move to confront the Ram. We make this

41

point to show the supreme power of the latter-day Persian (Iranian) empire.

A Self-Pleasing Beast

In the clause "But he did according to his will and became great," the Hebrew word "rason," translated "will," means "delight," "pleasure," "favor," "desire." Whatever the Ram desires he will do, and no one will hinder him. The Hebrew word translated "great" here is "gadowl" a causative word which should properly be rendered "caused to be great." HAW defines the term as follows (emphasis ours):

> The root is used for physical growth of people and other living things as well as for the increase of things tangible and intangible whether objects, sounds, feelings or authority...*it never refers to being numerous, only to being great in size, importance etc.*[12]

We sum up this section by noting that the Ram becomes a great power in the world by reason of his savagery and of the apparent weakness and/or hesitancy on the part of the rest of the world. His conquests indicate a despotic leader, driven by an exalted and haughty will, exerting that will with no apparent opposition for a time.

Persian History Since Alexander

Many changes have taken place in the area originally known as Persia since its defeat by Alexander the Great. Upon Alexander's death, the territory he had conquered was divided among three of his generals. Persia went to Seleucus and his

42

descendants, a dynasty which ruled with only nominal interference for a three hundred year period called the Hellenistic Age, because of the cultural influence of Greece. But by the end of the third century B.C., Rome had made its entrance on the scene and by 30 B.C. had swallowed up the entire Mediterranean basin, including Egypt. The power of Rome kept the Persians at bay; but the fall of Rome in the fifth century A.D., permitted a revival of a strong Persia under the rule of the Sassanid dynasty.

In the seventh century A.D., Muhammad (570-632 A.D.) founded Islam and completely transformed the religious, political, and social organization of the Middle East. During the reign of the first four caliphs (632-661), Islam spread rapidly. The prophet Muhammad taught that any Moslem who died in battle for Islam was assured entrance into Paradise. This sanctification of warfare bred into the Arabs, already a fighting people, a fanatical courage that proved well-nigh irresistible.[13] The Moslem victory in the Near East can be partly accounted for by the long series of wars between the Byzantine and Persian Empires...Moslem forces first conquered Syria (in 636 A.D.), then wrested Iraq from the Persians and within ten years after Muhammad's death, conquered Persia itself. In the years that followed, Moslem expansion continued...they conquered Asia Minor but not Constantinople. In the west, they subdued the whole of North Africa and then crossed the Strait of Gibraltar into Spain. Moslems invaded south and central France, and were only turned back by Charles Martel in the decisive battle of Tours (732 A.D). Meanwhile, placement of the new Moslem capital at Baghdad, produced a Middle Eastern culture in which Persian influence dominated. According to the historical record,

The Abbasid dynasty marked the high tide of Islamic power and civilization. In the early years of the caliphate, the empire was greater in size than the domain of the Roman Caesars; it was the product of an expansion during which the Muslims had "assimilated to their creed, speech, and even physical type, more aliens than any stock before or since, not excepting the Hellenic, the Roman, the Anglo-Saxon or the Russian..." In the latter part of the tenth century, Turkish nomads, called Seljuks, migrated from Asia into the Abbasid lands, where they accepted Islam. The Seljuks then began to seize land from the Abbasids and, after annexing most of Persia, gained control of Bagdad in 1055 and absorbed Iraq. Later, the Seljuks conquered Syria and Palestine, and then proceeded to annex part of Asia Minor from the Byzantines. [14]

This great advance of the Seljuks was responsible for the first crusade in 1095 A.D.

Early in the 13th century, Genghis Khan united the nomads of Mongolia, swept down into Persia and Iraq, capturing Baghdad, slaying the caliph. Iraq fell into a state of collapse from which it did not recover until our own century, and the Mongol ruling class was eventually absorbed into the Muslim culture of Persia and Iraq[15]

This region then attracted the Ottoman Turks, who adopted Islam fanatically and gained control of the former Abbasid dominions. They also conquered much of Arabia, and all of North Africa as far west as Morocco. The Ottoman Empire lived on into the 20th Century, defeated only during the first World War.

At the end of World War I, British troops occupied most of the Middle East. There was a strong movement in British political circles to include Iran in the British sphere of influence which stretched from India to the Persian Gulf. Britain's foreign secretary instructed his envoy, Sir Percy Cox, to negotiate a treaty in Teheran that would assure Britain political favor. The Iranian parliament refused to ratify the treaty, and the British missions were eventually forced to leave Iran. After seven years of war, rebellion, and chaos, Iran at last regained its independence.

In 1921, Iran concluded a treaty of friendship with the Soviet Union, but before it could be signed, Reza Khan staged a coup and rose rapidly to power. On December 13, 1925, the Iranian parliament, the Majlis, proclaimed him Shah of Iran, and a new dynasty, the Pahlavi, came into power. During the second World War, both Great Britain and the Soviet Union regained the ascendency in Iran. Reza Shah abdicated in favor of his young son, Mohammed Reza Pahlavi, and left Iran for South Africa where he died in 1944.

The more recent history of Iran has been one of increasing turmoil. The government was insecure because of so much internal struggle for power among rival factions. The period between 1953 and 1963 was one of turbulence with the Shah working to gain and perpetuate his power against various sources of opposition and dissent. Lenczowski sums up this decade of Iran's history:

45

The right wing groups, mostly representing big landowners who looked with hostility upon the Shah's land reform and other progressive ideas, were by and large successfully out-maneuvered by 1963, and after some violent demonstrations against the Shah's reform program, which included proposals to give women the right of political participation, the religious opposition was also effectively overcome. Its main spokesman, Ayatollah Khomeini, was deported from Iran...The Shah issued an imperial decree dissolving the Majlis in May 1961. For two and a half years the government of Iran continued without a parliament. The Shah took full advantage of this situation to press for a bold reform program.[16]

Oil revenues in the 1960s and 1970s financed these reforms, and allowed the Shah to strengthen Iran's military with weaponry purchased from the United States. But opposition and open defiance--both of the reforms and of the Shah himself--began in 1978 under the influence of religious dissenters, particularily from the exiled Ayatollah Khomeini. Khomeini denounced the Shah, calling for demonstrations and for the Shah's death. On January 19, 1979 the Shah and his family left Iran, and in February Khomeini returned in triumph from Paris. Dying of cancer in exile, the Shah never returned to Iran. On March 30, 1979 Khomeini, exercising supreme authority, declared Iran to be an Islamic republic. It is an excellent example of a theocracy, a state in which religious rulers who claim to represent their God hold all power, political and religious. As Lenczowski explains:

The new government revealed its foreign policy

preferences soon after the seizure of power. These were: nonalignment (as contrasted with the Shah's pro-American stance), support for the PLO, hostility toward Israel (a ban proclaimed on oil exports to it), withdrawal from an active role in the Persian Gulf, and close relationships with Islamic states (especially with Libya because of its early support to Khomeini) ...The army was demoralized after some sixty percent of its conscripts deserted and its top command underwent a bloody purge. Iran's borders were virtually defenseless.[17]

This chaos in Iran, rendering the nation vulnerable, encouraged Iraq to invade in an attempt to gain territory and Iran's oil fields. A bloody eight- year war ensued, ending in a stalemate. Although Khomeini died in June, 1989, Iran is still ruled today by a radical Islamic Fundamentalist government, with its parliament, the Majlis, composed principally of Moslem religious leaders. Having ruled the Islamic world once, Iran will endeavor to do so again as Daniel's vision warns us.

The escalating provocations between the Arabic-speaking world and the Western world will incite the Goat nations composed of the descendants of Javan, to run on the Ram to eliminate the perceived threat. While the Goat will achieve initial success in this conflict, the central power of the nations he symbolizes will then be "broken" (Daniel 8:8). In the power vacuum created by the dissolution of both of these world powers, the "four notable ones" will make their appearance, dividing the earth into the four distinct spheres of influence described in Daniel 7: that of Shem, Ham, Japheth, and the "diverse beast." In the next chapter, we will both identify and provide the scriptural description of those who make up the kingdom of the Goat.

End Notes

1. HAW, page 275
2. Ibid, page 290
3. ISBE, page 992
4. Unger, page 298
5. BDB, page 753
6. HAW, page 816
7. Ibid, page 146
8. Ibid, page 34
9. ISBE, page 2336
10. Strong, page 76
11. Ibid, page 11
12. HAW, page 151
13. Keil & Delitzsch, page 290
14. Wallbank, Taylor, Bailkey, page 176
15. Ibid, page 178
16. Lenczowski, page 210
17. ibid, 228-229

Chapter 3

The Goat

Daniel 8:5   And as I was considering, behold, an he goat came from the west on the face of the whole earth, and touched not the ground: and the goat had a notable horn between his eyes.

What follows the description of the Ram in Daniel's vision is the appearance of a mighty goat. While farmers often graze both sheep and goats together, because goat's are likely to gore and butt the sheep and injure them, the animals must be put in separate folds for the night. Like the ram, the goat is a symbol of aggressive strength. His vision of the Ram had caused Daniel some concern; the appearance of the belligerent Goat now added to that concern.

As I Was Considering

We noted in the previous chapter that the last clause of verse 2 began with "And I, I was," a phrase whose double personal pronoun emphasizes Daniel's involvement in the vision. Similarly, verse 5 opens with the same emphatic construction, "And I, I was considering"... The word "considering," is a Hebrew participle "mebin" which is used as a noun for emphasis and which means to "understand, consider, perceive, or regard." We know from the outset of verse 5 that Daniel must have been in deep concentration at this point in his vision. Of the Hebrew "mebin," HAW tells us that:

There are seventeen other renderings in addition. (ASV almost the same: RSV varies the readings for the two most numerous, "understand" and "consider" by interchanging "perceive," "observe," et all.). The verb and its derivatives are used 247 times. Its main English usage is "understanding" or "insight." The background idea of the verb is to "discern," and this lies behind the derivative nouns and the close relation derived from substantive *bayin* from which comes the preposition *ben* "between." The combination of these words, "discern between" is used in I Kgs 3:9, "That I may discern between good and evil." *Ben* includes the concept of distinguishment that leads to understanding. The verb refers to knowledge which is superior to the mere gathering of data. It can also mean "to be perceptive" (Ps 73:22).[1]

Rather than just idly "considering," then (as the English translation suggests), Daniel's word choice in verse 5 emphasizes his attempt to discern mentally what the Ram and the attendant circumstances implied. We, too, should learn to sift spiritual facts as Daniel did, if we are to draw God-given conclusions. HAW defines understanding as follows:

> While understanding is a gift of God, it does not come automatically. The possession of it requires a persistent diligence. It is more than IQ; it connotes character. One is at fault if he doesn't have it and in fact, not to pursue it will incur God's punishment (Prov 2:1f; Ruth 1:2f.). When one acts on the objective presentations of God's revelation, he will attain the ideal of the

significance of understanding.[2]

God-given understanding is of such importance that it must be diligently sought. Indeed, one of the primary objectives of our writing is to encourage God's people to actively pursue a correct understanding of the Scriptures. To their detriment, many believers are content to accept the teaching of others rather than personally, diligently, to engage in study that is accompanied by God's blessing. Timothy exhorts all of us:

II Timothy 2:15 Be diligent to show yourself approved (tested and passed the test) unto God, a workman that does not need to be ashamed, (naked before God) rightly dividing (cutting a straight furrow by means of) the word of truth.

Likewise, we urge our readers to stop and consider, to try to understand (discern) what God may be saying in a personal way through the Scriptures. While Daniel was viewing the scene of the Ram and sifting out its meaning, God added another element to his vision.

An He Goat Came From The West

Just as the characteristics of the "beasts out of the sea" cited in chapter seven of Daniel are descriptive of the nations they symbolize, so the properties of the Goat describe the nations it symbolizes. ISBE describes the chief characteristics of goats as follows:

Domestic goats differ greatly among themselves in the color and length of their hair, in the size and shape of their horns, which are usually larger in the males, but in some breeds may be absent in both sexes. A very constant feature in both wild and domestic goats is the bearded chin of the male. The goats of Palestine and Syria are usually black (Cant 4:1), though sometimes partly or entirely white or brown... They are herded in large numbers in the mountainous or hilly districts, and vie with their wild congeners in climbing into apparently impossible places. They feed not only on herbs, but also on shrubs and small trees, to which they are most destructive...They are responsible for the deforested condition of Judaea and Lebanon.[3]

This portrait of goats consuming all vegetation in their path indicates their potential destructiveness. Further, goats are by nature unpredictable, using their horns not only to defend themselves but to demonstrate aggression. Excellent fighters when provoked, goats use their horns as deadly instruments to rip and tear their enemies. In the composition of a goat herd, a single leader, usually one of the older goats, always holds the group together. That leader is trained to keep near the goatherd and not to eat as long as he wears the bell. The necessity for a strong leader among a group of aggressive, unpredictable, and destructive nations will become all too apparent as we consider those the goat symbolizes.

Verse 5 continues, "behold an he goat came from the west." As we stated in a previous chapter, the interjection translated "behold" denotes a special sight or way of seeing the divine illumination that was unfolding before Daniel's eyes. The word "he" is interposed into the text to signify that Daniel saw a male goat--a deduction made by commentators determined to identify the Goat with Alexander the Great. Most commentaries then ignore the plural adjective that describes the Goat. The adjective "azaz" is a prime root which means "to be stout" (lit. or fig.): harden, impudent, prevail, strengthen (self), be strong."[4] From this root, the word derives the meaning "vehement, harsh, fierce, greedy, mighty, power, roughly."[5] But it is the *plural form of this adjective modifying "Goat" that is the key to its symbolic significance. Since the Hebrew adjective always agrees with the noun it modifies in gender, number and case,*[6] the word unit, "tsaphiry-haeziym," is properly translated "strong or mighty *Goats*." The presence of the plural adjective makes the word "Goat" plural as well, even though the noun itself does not have a plural ending. The one symbolic Goat represents a herd of strong and mighty *Goats* that will run on the Ram; and, as in the case of the Ram, the Goat, too, represents nations. We note that Jesus, too, used sheep and goats to denote nations whose people either worship God or reject Him, as seen in the following:

> Matthew 25:32　And before him shall be gathered all nations: and he shall separate them one from another, as a shepherd divideth his sheep from the goats.

The fact that the goats Daniel mentions in verse 5 came from the west indicates that they symbolize nations of the Western world, specifically the descendants of Javan as we will discuss later in identifying the Goat with the "King of Graecia" seen in verse 21. The use of the Hebrew word for "west" connotes "the region of the evening sun." From the vantage point of the Hebrews along the extreme south eastern coast of the Mediterranean, the west referred to the area of the Mediterranean west of Israel. In Daniel's time, as even today, this was primarily the territory of the descendants of Javan.

On The Face Of The Whole Earth

In the phrase "On the face of the whole earth," the words translated "on the face of" come from the Hebrew expression "al paniy," whose usage Brown, Driver, and Briggs define as follows:

> "Al paniy" has different meanings according to the different senses of the noun and the prep.: a. From the sense of face or front: (a) in front of... b. From the sense of surface, Gen 1:2 upon the face of the deep.[7]

To render such an expression properly, the translator must base his choice on the context. From the above quote, definition (a) "in front of" seems most consistent with the text: The goats do not attack upon the "face of the whole earth," but their attack *is observed* or occurs *"in front of"* all the people of the earth. We based our decision to render the phrase this way partly on the proper translation of the phrase which follows.

And Touched Not The Ground

Translated literally, the phrase reads: "And there is not lay hand upon in the earth." HAW gives the meaning of the Hebrew word translated "there is not" in this passage as follows:

> "Ayin," translated "there is not" is basically a negative substantive used most to negate a noun or noun clause. The negative concept is always present wherever the word is used.[8]

In the original language, then, this phrase does not convey the idea that the Goat (usually identified as Alexander the Great) will move so rapidly in his conquest that his feet won't have time to touch the ground as some commentaries suggest! Instead, the force of the phrase is that no nation in the earth will oppose the operation of the nations of Javan when they attack the Ram. This reading is substantiated further by the meaning of the Hebrew word "naga" translated "touched" in this passage. The word "naga" a prime root; meaning "to touch, i.e., to lay the hand upon (for any purpose;...); violently, to strike [punish, defeat, destroy, etc."])[9] suggests that in all the earth, none will be inclined to strike, punish, or lay a hand upon these goats.[1]

And The Goat Had A Notable Horn Between His Eyes

Oddly, Daniel tells us that the animal he saw "had

---

[1] A good illustration of the inability of any one to "touch" the goat was seen in the recent war with Iraq. No nation in the world could have stood against the allied coalition with its overpowering superiority. This coalition was not the "Goat" but a force similiar to it will destroy the Ram.

a notable horn between his eyes." Since goats characteristically have two horns, and since the horn is a symbol of power and authority, a single horn on the mighty Goat probably symbolizes a consolidation of power. Davis confirms this use of the symbol elsewhere in Scripture;

> Horn denotes political power, the image being drawn from bulls which push with their horns (Psa cxxxii. 17; Jer xlviii. 25), and in prophetic language signifies a kingdom (Dan. Vii.8,11,21; Zech 1. 18,19) or kings (Rev.xvii.12,16).[10]

With such symbolism in mind, we find in Daniel's vision many western nations assembled under a central power to destroy the Ram.

The KJV describes the Goat's horn as "notable," a word derived from the Hebrew "chazuwth" which comes from a root meaning "to gaze at, mentally to perceive, contemplate (with pleasure); spec. to have a vision of: behold, look, prophesy, provide, see."[11] "Chazuwth" then describes a figure of striking appearance, a revelation, or (by impl) a compact, agreement, notable (one), vision.[12] Commentators have advanced many diverse opinions as to the meaning of this word as it is applied to the Goat. The Cambridge Bible notes[13] suggest that the phrase means a "horn of sight." Keil and Delitzsch hold that the meaning of "chazuth" is as follows:

> The goat had between its eyes "qeren Chazuwth"; i.e., not a "horn of vision," a horn such as a goat naturally has, but here only in vision (Hofm., Klief.). This interpretation would render "Chazuwth" an altogether useless

addition, since the goat itself, only in vision, is described as it appeared in the vision. For the right explanation of the expression reference must be made to ver. 8, where, instead of horn of vision, there is used the expression "Chazuwth hagadolah" (the great horn).[14]

If, as Keil concludes, the word "chazuwth" denotes "a horn of sight, consideration, of considerable greatness,"[15] the single horn must symbolize the consolidation of tremendous power and control which will be observed by people the world over. This consolidation does not mean that Daniel's vision referred to only one nation. As we have already noted, the plural adjective which modifies the word "goat" in the original text points to several nations, subject to a single leader, just as a herd of goats is led by a single "lead" goat. The validity of a single leader is further confirmed in verse 21 where the "great horn" is designated the "first king." He wears the bell.

And He Came To The Ram That Had Two Horns

As Daniel watched, the Goat of his vision attacked and destroyed the Ram. Literally, the first clause of verse 6 reads, "He came until the ram." "Until" comes from the Hebrew "ad," a word which emphasizes continuity: continuous existence of nations (Isaiah 47:7), continuous relations between God and his people (I Chronicles 28:9, Isaiah 64:8, Micah 7:18).[16] HAW explains the word as follows (emphasis ours):

'Ad I. Perpetuity. ASV, RSV translate similarly, except in Isa 45:17. Here the former has "world without end" while the latter has "to all

57

eternity"...Frequently the word 'ad is applied to God. His existence is eternal (Isa 57:15)...This word is also applied to Israel. The Davidic dynasty will continue forever, depending upon their response to the covenant (Psa 111:3; 112:3;)...*This word is used temporally to indicate a continuation of an event from a point in the past to the present* (Gen 19:37-38).[17]

With this definition in mind, we must adjust our thinking to the fact that *this word refers to the antiquity of the empire symbolized by the Ram and its continuence to the present day.* This premise is further bolstered by Gabriel's statement in verse 17 that, "at the time of the end shall be the vision."

The next phrase of the sentence (translated in the KJV, "that had two horns") is literally "lord of the horns." Translated from "ba'al," this Hebrew word means "owner," *lord*, of the land, in Job 31:39; of the ass, in Isaiah 1:3; of goods, in Ecclesiastes 5:10; of riches, in Ecclesiastes 5:12...[18] The entire sentence to this point would therefore read, "He came until the ram lord (owner) of the horns." Remembering that in Scripture horns express power, strength, or authority, this entire sentence indicates that the Ram possessed his power and strength from ancient times and that, as "lord of the horns," he maintains these qualities into the present.

Which I Had Seen Standing Before The River

The clause that follows, "Which I had seen standing before the river" literally reads, "Which I saw standing to the face of the mourner," with "mourner" translated from the same Hebrew word "'abal" seen in verse 2, a prime root which means to bewail, lament, or mourn.[19]

And Ran Unto Him In The Fury Of His Power

In the final clause of the verse, "And ran unto him in the fury of his power," the verb "ruwts" as used here and translated "ran," denotes the idea of haste, or hurry. The reason for the haste was passion, generated by the animosity with which the Goats viewed the Ram. The word translated " fury" comes from the Hebrew word "chema" which means heat, fig., anger, hot displeasure, indignation, rage, wrath (ful).[20] According to Daniel's vision, then, the Goat ran (rushed) in the fury (anger, wrath, heat) of his power (strength, violence).

When Iraq suddenly invaded Kuwait on August 2, 1990, the United States immediately sent troops to protect Saudi Arabia from invasion. After some deliberation, the Security Council of the United Nations condemned Iraq for this attack, voting to invoke economic sanctions against the nation. Only after repeated deliberations did the Security Council grant permission for the massed troops of 24 nations to drive Iraq's army out of Kuwait. Such a delay will not occur when the Goat runs on the Ram. So much anger and passion to destroy the Ram will be generated by the Western nations that haste will be the order of that day. It is frightening to reflect on what event or series of events could prompt such a response.

As "lord of the horns," Iran is already guilty of provoking the Western nations. Their act of taking hostage the employees of the American Embassy in Teheran in 1979 and their involvement in terrorism in Lebanon and in Europe has turned world opinion against them. The news services recently reported that Iran paid terrorists in Lebanon to take the hostages in Beirut and was involved in the bombing of the U.S. Marine barracks at the Beirut airport in 1983. They have already been playing a dangerous political game and recent disclosures of their military expansion point to some future confrontation.

At present, Iran is said to be spending billions of dollars for up-to-date arms from China, South Africa, North Korea, and Israel. It was also recently reported by the news services that Iran is buying surplus military equipment from the former Soviet military machine at greatly reduced prices, and that these purchases began even while Gorbachev was still in power. While such sales are not entirely unexpected (with governments that came out of the now-defunct Soviet Union in need of hard currency for world trade), Iran's rearmament nevertheless is the first drumbeat of danger. According to the Fort Worth Star-Telegram, November 29, 1992:

> Iran is shedding the moderate image it has sought to acquire in the last few years and is spreading revolutionary tentacles once again while rebuilding its military power...As in the days of Ayatollah Ruhollah Khomeini, the late revolutionary patriarch, Iran is throwing its political weight and oil money behind Islamic militants across the Arab world, from Algeria to Sudan...Gulf Arabs are alarmed at Iran's annexation in August, 1992 of Abu Musa, a tiny but strategic island at the mouth of the Strait of

Hormuz, the choke point for gulf tanker traffic...With Iraq defanged, Israel now also considers Iran to be its main enemy.[21]

The West can no more afford to have Iran the dominant force in the Middle East than it could Iraq.

While admittedly speculative, one theory about what will inspire the conflict Daniel described is not hard to imagine. The single issue of supreme importance to the West and over which Iran could conceivably exert control is oil--the life blood of the Western nations, and of Japan as well. Peaceful cooperation with the oil-rich Middle East states is vital to the West's maintaining power in the world. The United States imports over 50% of its oil, Europe and Japan far more than that proportion, from the Middle East. By dominating that region and controlling the flow of oil to the rest of the world, Iran could create an intolerable situation for the West. The raising of oil prices to astronomical levels would bankrupt the industrial nations. If Iran attempts extortion against the West over oil, those nations, many of whose people descended from Javan (who originally settled around the Mediterranean basin but then migrated north through France and into the British Isles) will act quickly. Or, if Moslems attempt to invade Europe through the Balkans, or even pose a nuclear threat, the United Nations will exercise no restraint to prevent Western retaliation.

He Was Moved With Anger Against Him

According to Daniel's vision in verse 7, the Goat "was moved with choler (fury) against him and smote the ram, and brake his two horns." "Fury" here is translated from the Hebrew word "chemah," meaning "heat; fig., anger, poison (from its fever) hot displeasure, furious (ly, ry), indignation, rage, wrath(ful)."[22]   Ezekiel used this same word to describe Israel after their defeat by Babylon:

> Ezekiel 19:12 But she was plucked up in *fury*, she was cast down to the ground, and the east wind dried up her fruit: her strong rods were broken and withered; the fire consumed them.
>
> 13 And now she is planted in the wilderness, in a dry and thirsty ground.

This passage from Ezekiel portrays the end of the siege of Jerusalem in 586 B.C., when only the old, the crippled, and the derelicts remained of God's people in Judah. Both the city of Jerusalem and the Temple were destroyed and the land left desolate. When the fury of the Goat is released on the Ram, the Ram, too, will be completely destroyed, since verse 7 ends with the solemn declaration that "there was none that could deliver the ram out of his hand."

The He-Goat Grew Very Great And...The Great Horn Was Broken

We read in verse 8 that the tremendous display of power against the Ram only increased the Goat's power: "Therefore the he-goat waxed very great." But in the zenith of his power ("and when he was strong," from the Hebrew stative verb "asam" meaning "to be mighty, numerous, strong"), at a time when the Goat seemed invincible, "the great horn was broken." The

62

Hebrew verb "broken" comes from a prime root meaning "to burst, (lit. or fig.,): break (down, off, in pieces) ...crush, destroy, hurt..."[23] We see then that the Goat's vast array of power, his numbers, and his might when he stamps the Ram will explode, shattering the centralized power of the goat nations.

And For It Came Up Four Notable Ones

With the authority and power of the Goat shattered the vision continues, "And for it came up four notable ones toward the four winds of heaven." This is a good translation of the passage. Literally it would read, "four conspicuous horns ascend toward the four winds of heaven." Here the emphasis is on the global aspect of these "horns" or seats of power. Unlike the Ram, whose kingdom is utterly destroyed in the conflict, the Goat loses only his *horn*. And since the horn is the symbol of authority, the implication is that the goat nations as national entities will continue, but without their "first king" (verse 21). These nations will eventually join with other descendants of Japheth to become *one* of the "four notable ones" (kingdoms) of Daniel 7:5 and Daniel 8:22--the kingdom of the sons of Japheth. And while the destruction of the Ram's empire will create a power vacuum in the Middle East, that vacuum will quickly be filled by the rise of the Semitic coalition symbolized by the lion with eagle's wings of Daniel 7:4.[2] Daniel 7 introduces us to these four kingdoms (beasts) representing regions of the world extending "to the four winds of heaven." Daniel 8 tells us how they come into existence and

---

[2] See our book, *The Four Beasts Of Daniel 7*, for details.

63

their significance in the "little horn's" final world empire.

Identification Of The Goat

In Daniel 8:21 we find that "The rough goat is the king of Grecia,"with the word "rough" translated from a prime root, "sa'ar," which means "to storm; by impl. to shiver, i.e., fear--be (horribly) afraid, fear, hurl as a storm, be tempestuous, come like (take away as with) a whirlwind."[24]   The Goat exhibited these "rough" instincts when he "stormed" against the Ram in a fit of tempestuous wrath.

As "king of Grecia" the traditional interpretation identifies this "king of Grecia" in the KJV with Alexander the Great, but the text does not demand that the Goat represent only Greece under Alexander the Great. In fact, several facts militate against this interpretation. We will consider those facts under two principal categories: who is the "king of Grecia" and when does he mount the stage of history?

The King Of Grecia--Who Is He?

The word translated "Grecia" in the KJV is simply the Hebrew word "Javan," identified in Genesis 10:2 as the fourth son of Japheth. Although Japheth had seven sons, the biblical record is restricted to the posterity of Gomer and Javan.[3] It is from the heirs of these two sons of Japheth that the "enlargement" of Japheth predicted in Genesis 9:27 begins and is, for the most part, carried forward; for in the course of later

---

[3] See Genesis 10:4.

history the descendants of both sons played major roles in the colonization of the rest of the world. Very early these two major divisions (sons of Javan and Gomer) settled in Europe. Gomer migrated into the central and eastern areas of Europe, while Javan took possession of the entire northern and western coast of the Mediterranean and the "islands of the sea" (Genesis 10:5; Isaiah 11:11). Ancient history offers the following account of the extent of Javan's influence:

> The Greeks and Romans were offshoots of a common Indo-European stock, and settlement of the Greek and Italian peninsulas followed stages that were broadly parallel. Between 2000 and 1000 B.C., when Indo-European peoples invaded the Aegean world, a western wing of this nomadic migration filtered into the Italian peninsula, then inhabited by indigenous Neolithic tribes. The first invaders, skilled in the use of copper and bronze, settled in the Po valley. There followed another wave of Indo-European tribes, the Italic people, who were equipped with iron weapons and tools; in time, the newer and older settlers intermingled and spread throughout the peninsula.[25]

Civilization, Past and Present establishes Javan as in control of the entire Mediterranean basin:

> After the eighth century, Greek (Ionian) colonists established city-states in southern Italy, known as Magna Graecia (Greater Greece), and in Sicily. The Greeks disseminated the achievements of Hellenic culture... Sicily and Greater Greece also served as a protective buffer against powerful and

prosperous Carthage, the Phoenician colony established in North Africa around 800 B.C. No one at the time would have believed that the future of the entire Mediterranean belonged to an insignificant Latin village on the Tiber River, then in the shadow of Etruscan expansion. Here was Rome, destined to be ruler of the ancient world.[26]

Since Daniel's prophecy extends to "the four winds of heaven," suggesting the farthest reaches of the earth, clearly Daniel's vision anticipated a much larger sphere than just Greece. We may realistically conclude that the Goat will be composed of those Western nations descended primarily from Javan.

The proper identification of Daniel's "Grecia" aside, a second fact militates against the theory that the Goat represents Greece under Alexander the Great.

The "King Of Grecia"--When Is He?

Precisely, Daniel 8:17 and 19 tell us that the events of the vision are for the *time of the end.* Under a dual fulfillment (for which there is no textual proof) imposed on this passage, the evidence from the text, itself, rules out identification of the horn of the Goat with Alexander the Great. In addition, in verse 26, Gabriel tells Daniel to "shut thou up the vision; for it shall be for many days." The word "shut" means "to keep hidden or secret". Daniel received this vision less than a year before Cyrus took control of the Median kingdom in his consolidation of Medo-Persia and only 13 years before he invaded Babylon; why, then, would the prophet be directed to "shut" his vision, with the fulfillment of the Ram's campaigns on

66

his doorstep, so to speak? Granted, some time was still to pass before Alexander would appear on the scene, but the phrase "it shall be for many days" suggests a longer duration than what preceded Alexander's reign. The implication of the "many days' is underscored in verse 23 by the phrase "when the transgressors are come to the full" and again by the appearance of "the king of fierce countenance"--almost universally accepted as a reference to the Antichrist.

Three additional facts which cast doubt on the horn's identification with Alexander the Great remain to be mentioned before we conclude this chapter. Since Alexander's exploits took place during the intertestamental period when God was silent to Israel, giving no revelation, we must therefore assume that knowledge of the events of this period is not vital to *our understanding of His plan for the ages.*

Also, as we observed earlier, the Goat was fierce, and goats must be separated from the flock for the safety of others of the flock. Scripturally, goats symbolize aggressive and belligerent power, and are destructive of the land they inhabit. All the sons of Japheth, but especially Javan and Gomer, have colonized much of the land mass of the world, conquering and exploiting both Hamites and Semites.

Finally, the "Goat" described in Daniel 8 symbolizes several nations, not just one. The second part of verse 21 identifies the great horn between the eyes of the Goat as the "first king," with the word "first" translated from the Hebrew "ri'shown" which denotes the "first of many, head, chief, leader."[27] HAW makes this observation about the word:

"Ri'shon." First, primary (ordinal number)...The word occurs 180 times in the OT...The overwhelming number of occurrences are best translated "former," "first" of two, of time (Gen 25:25)...The next most common usage is in the sense of "first," as in "first" of mankind (Job 15:7); "first" day of a ritual (Deut 16:4); "first" to fall in battle (I Sam 14:14)...[28]

Thus, the great horn between the eyes of the Goat symbolizes the primary leader in the goat nations' power and authority.

Considering the implication of the Goat's identification with the modern West, the following statement in the text, "the great horn was broken" is sobering. As we have previously noted, the word "broken" comes from the Hebrew word "shabar" a prime root meaning "to burst (lit. or fig.):-break (down, off, in pieces, up), broken ([hearted]),...crush, destroy, hurt, quench, ruin,"[29] According to HAW:

> ...Here the verb is used to describe judgmental, punitive activity. Often such action is levelled against non-covenant peoples: the king of Babylon, Jer 28:2; the Pharoah, Ezek 30:21; Damascus, Amos 1:5; Elam, Jer 49:35; Assyrians, Isa 14:25; Nebuchadnezzar, Jer 28:11.[30]

Thus, Scripture warns us that the "notable" horn, representing the power and authority of the leader of the goats will be destroyed, and this destruction may be accurately perceived as judgmental and punitive on God's part against those nations making up the goat.

The recent breakup of the Soviet Union was an indispensable part of the fulfillment of this prophecy in God's timetable. The Soviet Union would never have allowed another power equivalent to that of the goat nations to attack near its borders. Even during the recent revolution in Iran, the Soviet government asserted itself: on November 19, 1978, Soviet President Brezhnev warned the United States against interfering in the internal affairs of Iran.[31] With the collapse of the Soviet Union and the rise of a well-armed Iran, all elements are moving into place for a fulfillment of this prophecy. Iran emerged from the recent Gulf war as the predominant power in the region, excluding Israel. Their destruction by the Goat will signal that the world is on the threshold of the end times revealed in the book of Daniel.

End Notes

1. HAW, page 103
2. Ibid, page 104
3. ISBE, page 1249
4. Strong, page 87
5. Ibid, page 86
6. Davidson, page 44
7. BDB, page 818
8. HAW, page 37
9. Strong, page 76
10. Davis, page 323
11. Strong, page 38
12. Ibid, page 38
13. Cambridge Bible, page 1118
14. Keil & Delitzsch, page 292
15. Ibid, page 292
16. BDB, page 723
17. HAW, pages 645-646

18. BDB, page 127
19. Strong, page 7
20. Ibid, page 40
21. Fort Worth Star Telegram, Nov. 29, 1992
22. Strong, page 40
23. Ibid, page 112
24. Ibid, page 119
25. Wallbank, Taylor, Bailkey, page 65
26. Ibid, page 65
27. BDB, page 911
28. HAW, page 826
29. Strong, page 112
30. HAW, page 901
31. Lenczowski, page 226

Chapter 4

The Four Notable Ones

Daniel 8:8 Therefore the he goat waxed very great: and when he was strong, the great horn was broken; and for it came up four notable ones toward the four winds of heaven.

We saw in the previous chapter that the Goat with its tremendous power will be able to cast the Ram to the ground (Daniel 8:7), but afterward, the great horn between the eyes of the Goat will be broken. Symbolizing a kingdom composed of the descendants of Javan, the Goat will continue to exist but without the authority and power of the "first king." In the power vacuum to follow the demise of the Goat's power, we read in Daniel's prophecy the rise of four "notable ones," (four other horns which symbolize four kingdoms) "toward the four winds of heaven" (8:8). The phrase "four winds of heaven" not only indicates that the kingdoms represented by these four "notable ones" will be world-wide in scope but this is the same phrase the prophet used in 7:2 to refer to the four great beasts that came up from the sea and for a third time in Daniel 11:4 to establish the world-wide realm of the "mighty king," whose kingdom will be broken and "divided toward the four winds of heaven." The repetition of this unusual phrase is an interpretive key *linking all three passages together on the same subject.* Daniel 7 introduces the four kingdoms as beasts emerging from the entire "sea" of humanity (cf. Revelation 17:14). Daniel 8 tell how they come into existence as the result of a struggle between the empire of a Ram and a coalition of Goat nations. Daniel 11 picks up the account at the same event, the demise of the Goat's power when his great horn is broken. Each instance fills in progressively more detail of the end-time and how those details involve Daniel's people, Israel.

Biblical evidence does not support the view that the "four notable ones" mentioned in Daniel 8 result from the division of Alexander's empire after his death. To the contrary, the Scriptures state that the kingdoms resulting from the break-up of the kingdom of Javan and their "first king" (whoever that may be) were established, "but not in his power" (Daniel 8:22). The passage in Daniel 11 also disassociates the "mighty king" from the subsequent four kingdoms (emphasis ours):

Daniel 11:4 And when he shall stand up, his kingdom shall be broken, and shall be divided toward the four winds of heaven; and *not to his posterity, nor according to his dominion which he ruled*: for his kingdom shall be plucked up, even for others beside those.

Not only do the Scriptures remind us that these events are to occur in *the time of the end* and are thus yet future (see Daniel 8:17,19,26), they specifically point out that the four kingdoms do *not* result from anything the notable horn of the Goat has done. With respect to Alexander the Great, Daniel 11:4 above would refer to the territory he conquered ("dominion"). Speaking of the same four kingdoms mentioned in Daniel 7:2 Keil points out that:

The four winds stand in relation to the four quarters of the heavens: cf. Jer. xlix. 39...The winds of the heavens represent the heavenly powers and forces by which God sets the nations of the world in motion; and the number four has a symbolical meaning: that the people of all regions of the earth are moved hither and thither in violent commotion.[1]

This alone rules out Alexander the Great's empire since the kingdoms that emerged after his death were not world-wide in scope.

The Identity Of The Four Notable Ones

Let us rehearse the progressive unveiling of information in Scripture regarding the "four notable ones": Daniel 7:2b-3 introduces these four kingdoms as beasts: "behold, the four winds of the heaven strove upon the great sea, and four great beasts came up from the sea, diverse one from another"; Daniel 7:17 adds that "these great beasts, which are four, are four kings, which shall arise out of the earth"; Daniel 8:8 continues to identify these four great kingdoms which extend to the "four winds of heaven" by explaining their origin, that they are the end result of a savage conflict between an aggressive ram and wrathful goats led by an extremely strong leader. Daniel 8:21-22 continue this identification, which is subsequently confirmed by the angelic messenger, Gabriel:

Daniel 8:21 And the rough goat is the king of Grecia (Javan): and the great horn that is between his eyes is the first king.

22 Now that being broken, whereas four

stood up for it, four kingdoms shall stand up out of the nation, but not in his power.

After having assured Daniel in chapter 10 verse 14 that, "I am come to make thee understand what shall befall thy people in the latter days; for yet the vision is for many days," Gabriel resumes the subject of these four kingdoms in Daniel 11, adding still more detail:

Daniel 11:2 And now will I shew thee the truth. Behold, there shall stand up yet three kings in Persia; and the fourth shall be far richer than they all, and by his strength through his riches he shall stir up all against the realm of Grecia (Javan).

3 And a mighty king shall stand up, that shall rule with great dominion, and do according to his will.

4 And when he shall stand up, his kingdom shall be broken, and shall be divided toward the four winds of heaven; and not to his posterity, nor according to his dominion which he ruled; for his kingdom shall be plucked up, even for others beside those.

The unifying phrase "the four winds of heaven" in all three visions (Daniel 7,8 and 11) is used to tie the subject matter of these four kingdoms together. Gabriel tells Daniel that after the elimination of the

Ram and the dissolution of the power of the Goat nations, four entities will arise. As we have seen, chapter seven describes these entities, while chapter eight explains how they will come to be: they constitute four kingdoms of nations polarized according to ancient ethnic lines--those of Shem, Ham, Japheth--and the "diverse beast" which will eventually assimilate the first three kingdoms. Shem's descendents will be united under one head, Japheth's under one head, Ham's under four heads; the "diverse beast" will have one head but ten horns. Assimilated into the final kingdom of the "little horn," the result will be a "diverse beast" indeed, exhibiting the mouth of the lion (Shem), the feet of the bear (Japheth), and the body of the leopard (Ham) (see Revelation 13:2).

The First Notable One

The first "notable one" is the same kingdom symbolized in Daniel 7:4 by the lion with eagle's wings. (For a comprehensive treatment of the four kingdoms, we would refer you to our book, *The Four Beasts of Daniel 7.*) The lion and the eagle characteristically represent the royalty of the animal and bird kingdoms, the lion as king of the jungle and the eagle as magistrate of the skies. The combination of these two creatures to symbolize one kingdom would seem to indicate that kingdom's supreme power over earth and sky. They portray a regal kingdom, powerful enough to dominate the earth and with God's enabling power, able to soar into the heavens. On a world-wide scale, this kingdom could only arise from the Semites, the descendants of Shem, to whom was entrusted the sacred responsibility of representing God among the families of the earth. This royal responsibility we call the theocractic rule, and those who were charged with maintaining God's representation in the earth, theocratic rulers. To review briefly how this system came to be, we must go back to man's beginning, to Adam, God's first theocratic ruler.

Since the theocracy is that rule on earth under the immediate direction of God, it involves man's dominion over all God's earthly creation. It is a stewardship in God's stead, carrying out oversight of the creation with the same care and concern that God would exercise, and mediating God's ordinances, statutes, and judgments to each generation of the human race. When Adam disobeyed God's direct command and repudiated the authority of his Creator, God announced the new theocratic program and ruler would come through the seed of woman. This was the first promise of an eternal theocratic ruler, the Lord Jesus Christ.

> Genesis 3:15 And I will put enmity between thee
> and the woman, and between thy
> seed and her seed; it shall bruise thy
> head, and thou shalt bruise his heel.

This early phase of the theocracy ended with the world-wide flood because mankind as a whole had refused the rule of God on earth. But we read in Genesis 6:8 that "Noah found grace in the eyes of the Lord." Noah and his family were delivered from the flood, establishing the patriarch as the first royal representative of God in the post-diluvian world, and God gave him instructions he was to pass on to all mankind. We call these instructions the Noahic covenant.

In Genesis 9, by bestowing the patriarchal blessing on both Shem and Japheth, Noah prophesied the course the theocracy would take in the ages to come:

Genesis 9:26 And he said, Blessed be the Lord God of Shem; and Canaan shall be his servant.

27 God shall enlarge Japheth, and he shall dwell in the tents of Shem; and Canaan shall be his servant.

Verse 26 should properly read, "Blessed be Shem of the Lord God." Shem's faithfulness to God would be rewarded by the blessings of God. And Japheth, too, was promised certain material blessings. While Ham received neither a special blessing nor a curse, Noah cursed Canaan, the one of Ham's sons who probably exhibited the flawed character of Ham more than any of the other's (See Ham's failure in Genesis 9:20-25). After Noah's death the theocratic position passed to his eldest son, Shem, and so on through Shem's descendants.

With the failure of mankind at the Tower of Babel, God further restricted the line of the theocracy. The right to rule was taken from the general descendants of Shem and placed in the hands of a single family (Genesis 11). From the line of Arphaxad, Shem's third son, God chose Abram of Ur of the Chaldees (whose name He later changed to Abraham) to be the theocratic ruler; through Abram's descendants the world was to be won for God's kingdom (Genesis 12). We must emphasize that the ultimate fulfillment of the theocracy will come through One who will be an eternal King.

Abraham gained his authority as the recipient of God's promises. In an unconditional covenant, God promised Abraham a land, a posterity, a name, and a universal blessing.

Genesis 12:2 And I will make of thee a great nation, and I will bless thee, and make thy name great: and thou shalt be a blessing.

3 And I will bless them that bless thee, and curse him that curseth thee: and in thee shall all families of the earth be blessed.

On Abraham's death, the theocratic rule passed to Isaac, and from Isaac to Jacob, whose name was subsequently changed to Israel. Jacob (or Israel) had twelve sons, and the theocratic rule passed on through Judah, Jacob's fourth son by Leah. Reuben lost his birthright as the eldest son because of incest, Simeon and Levi, the second and third sons, lost the ruling position because of their involvement in the murder of the Hivites at Shechem. The tribe of Judah thus became the designated line of the theocratic rulers under God in Israel. When the monarchy was established in the nation of Israel, the kings were chosen from the tribe of Judah, predicted in Jacob's blessing on his sons:

Genesis 49:10 The sceptre shall not depart from Judah, nor a lawgiver from between his feet, until Shiloh come; and unto him shall the gathering of the people be.

Pentecost makes this observation about the "Sceptre" mentioned in the passage above:

> There is a further reference to the anticipated fulfillment of this theocratic program in Numbers 24:17-19, where it is promised that the "Sceptre shall rise out of Israel." This "Sceptre" is the One in whom the authority resides, who will destroy His enemies and raise up Israel to prominence.[2]

The divine ideal of a true king, King David, of the tribe of Judah, appears all through Scripture as the perfect realization of the theocratic ruler. God made a covenant with David to established an eternal monarchy through his lineage:

II Samuel 7:8   Now therefore so shalt thou say unto my servant David, Thus saith the Lord of hosts, I took thee from the sheep-cote, from following the sheep, to be ruler over my people, over Israel.

12   And when thy days be fulfilled, and thou shalt sleep with thy fathers, I will set up thy seed after thee, which shall proceed out of thy bowels, and I will establish his kingdom.

16   And thine house and thy kingdom shall be established forever before thee: thy throne shall be established for ever.

Upon David's death, the theocratic rule passed to

his son Solomon, but after the death of Solomon, the kingdom divided with ten rebellious tribes forming the northern kingdom, Israel, and only two tribes left as a testimony to God's promise to David. These two tribes, Judah and Benjamin, became known as the southern kingdom, Judah. The line of the theocracy continued for some years in Judah beyond the kingdom of the rebellious tribes in the north, which God judged and delivered into the hands of the Assyrians in 722 B.C. Later, the failure of the southern kingdom resulted in its fall in 606 B.C., and the people were deported into Babylonian captivity. After 70 years of exile in Babylon, some of Judah returned to the land, lapsing into their former sinful ways. They intermarried with the heathen around them and instituted Judaism, the religion of the Pharisees, a counterfeit religion that opposed the Messiah when He came to set up the kingdom.

With the rejection of Christ, God placed his plans for these descendants of Shem and the theocracy on hold and made way for the intervening Church Age. The final and ideal form of the theocracy will be established when Christ comes the second time and sets up His kingdom by His power. Satan's counterfeit system established long ago at the Tower of Babel as a substitute for God's true theocracy, will be destroyed at the end of the Tribulation period when Christ returns to ascend the throne of David.

The Descendants Of Ishmael

Before going on to discuss the "second notable one," we should mention another group of Semites who will play a major role in the last days as part of the kingdom symbolized by the lion with eagle's wings. Part of the royal family from whom God has chosen His theocratic rulers are the descendants of Ishmael, the half-brother of Isaac and a son of Abraham by Hagar, Sarah's Egyptian maid. Like Jacob, Ishmael had 12 sons called princes ("nesyim,") to denote their royal heritage (Genesis 17:20; 25:16).

> Genesis 17:20 And as for Ishmael, I have heard thee: Behold, I have blessed him, and will make him fruitful, and will multiply him exceedingly; twelve princes shall he beget, and I will make him a great nation.
>
> 21 *But my covenant will I establish with Isaac.*

The envy and hatred of sibling rivalry established between Isaac and Ishmael so long ago continues between their modern descendants, both laying claim to the Promised Land and to status as God's chosen people. The religion of Ishmael's descendants, Islam, claims to be the world's only true religion. As Hatti explains:

> Ishmael's descendants have become great as a people. Around the name of the Arabs gleams that halo which belongs to the world-conquerors. Within a century after their rise this people became the masters of an empire extending from the shores of the Atlantic Ocean to the confines of China, an empire greater than that of Rome at its zenith. In this period of unprecedented expansion they "assimilated to their creed, speech, and even physical type, more aliens than any stock before or since, not excepting the Hellenic, the Roman, the

Anglo-Saxon, or the Russian."[3]

Because of Israel's priority, Ishmael's descendants do not play a dominant role in the Old Testament. They have, however, been prominent in the Middle East and in North Africa for generations. In the 7th century A.D., Muhammad (570-632), a direct descendant of Ishmael, founded a new religion called Islam, a word which means "submission" (to the will of Muhammad's god, Allah); Islam's followers called themselves Moslems, which means "those who have submitted." After an interim period of both struggle and rejection, Islam has become the most influential religion in the world. Moreover, during the last decade, Islam's converts have greatly exceeded Christianity's.

Moslems believe that the Koran, their Bible, contains the actual word of Allah (god) as revealed to Muhammad. Moslems hold the Koran so sacred that they do not encourage its translation into other languages fearing it may not be accurate. Wallbank, Taylor, and Bailkey explain:

> Because the Koran must never be used in
> translation for worship, the spread of Islam created
> a great deal of linguistic unity, which still remains
> today. Arabic supplanted many local languages as
> the language of daily use, and that part of the
> Muslim world which stretches from Morocco to
> Iraq is still Arabic-speaking. Furthermore, this
> book of the seventh century remains the last word
> on Muslim theology, law, and social institutions
> and is therefore still the most important textbook
> in Muslim universities.[4]

By establishing a counterfeit religion and a counterfeit theocracy, Islam has become Christianity's most formidable rival in the Church Age. Indeed, in the last days, Islamic fundamentalism will be the catalyst that polarizes the Semites, who are unified by their allegiance to Islam ("There is one God and Muhammad is his prophet"), and by their hatred for the West. This distrust of the West is seen in the following quotation from Time Magazine:

> Arab xenophobia, the abiding hatred of foreigners-especially Europeans and Americans--who have long divided, despoiled and dishonored the once powerful Arab world. Many Arabs share Saddam's complaint that the boundaries of the present-day Middle East were imposed arbitrarily by colonial rulers after World War I. And their anger was only intensified after World War II when Europe and America allowed another wave of usurpers, the Jews, to stake their ancient claim to Middle Eastern land. Regardless of their nationality, the Arabs still share an almost universal hatred of Israel as an aggressor and oppressor, and nothing since its founding has diminished that. Though these views may be exaggerated, even somewhat irrational, they are undeniably powerful.[5]

This unity on both religious and political grounds prevails throughout the Arab world, crossing even ethnic lines. While not of Ishmael's blood line, the Palestinians (descendants of Ham), Egyptians (descendants of Ham), Iranians (descendants of Japheth and Shem), and north Africans from such places as Ethiopia, Libya, the Sudan, etc. (descendants of Ham) have nevertheless largely converted to Islam and are now a part of the Pan-Arab league. When the Semites polarize, some of these nations (although not all) will join this kingdom of the lion with eagle's wings purely on the basis of a shared religion rather than on ethnic lines.

Shem had other children--Elam, Asshur, Lud, and Aram--whose families also settled in the Middle East, and whose ethnic identity has not been entirely lost. Abraham descended from Shem's third son, Arphaxad, and although some of Abraham's descendants have intermarried, thereby mingling the ethnic heritage of their descendants, when the Semites polarize into a kingdom after the Ram is destroyed, Ishmael's line will play the dominant role.[1] The kingdom of the first "notable one" will begin to assume a Semitic identity, the Lion with eagle's wings.

The Second Notable One

The second "notable one" who Daniel says, "came up toward the four winds of heaven" (Daniel 7:5), is represented by a bear, a symbol we identify with the Gentiles. As we have noted in an earlier chapter, Japheth's seven sons are listed in the Table of Nations (Genesis 10:1-5), emphasizing two of these sons, Gomer and Javan, by listing their sons. This same passage designates all of Japheth's descendants as "Gentiles":

---

[1] For more detail on the kingdom symbolized by the lion with eagles wings see our book, The Four Beasts of Daniel 7.

Genesis 10:5   By these were the isles of the
                Gentiles divided in their lands; every
                one after his tongue, and after their
                families, in their nations.

Secular history and geography along with Scripture demonstrate that the "enlargement of Japheth" predicted in Genesis 9:27 can be attributed primarily to the descendants of Gomer and Javan. Migrating far and wide, these two families were primarily responsible for Gentile occupation of the best land in an arc stretching from the tip of South America, through North America, Greenland, Iceland, across Europe, and then south to Australia and New Zealand. Other sons of Japheth settled much of Asia, including the area encompassed by Turkey, the former Soviet states, China, Japan, India, Iran, Afghanistan, Pakistan, and other nations of the far East. Japheth's descendants have thus taken in possession and/or governed three quarters of the globe.

Gentile participation in the Old Testament was minimal. Having been commissioned to maintain the theocracy, Semites, of course, played the dominant role in biblical history before the birth of Christ. After the gospels, which record the failure of the theocracy, the crucifixion of Christ, and the postponement of the kingdom, the Gentiles dominate the rest of the New Testament. The book of Acts records the transition--a change in emphasis from the Jews to the Gentiles, a change in the language in which Scripture was written, (from Hebrew to Greek), a shift from Jerusalem to Rome as the sacred city, from the age of law to the administration of grace, a change from the message of the kingdom to the gospel of grace and Gentiles proclaiming the message of God to the world in place of the Jews. With these alterations in God's earthly administration, the Gentiles began to shoulder the responsibility for spreading His Word, for winning a heavenly people instead of an earthly kingdom, and for "dwelling in the tents of Shem" (as predicted in Genesis 9:27). Their dominance since the destruction of Jerusalem in 70 A.D. confirms the Gentiles' present position of priority in God's plan for mankind. As a sign to Israel, our Lord predicted that Jerusalem would be occupied by the Gentiles until their "times be fulfilled":

> Luke 21:24 And they (Israel) shall fall by the edge of the sword, and shall be led away captive into all nations: and Jerusalem shall be trodden down of the Gentiles, until the times of the Gentiles be fulfilled.

This Gentile oversight of Jerusalem since 70 A.D. fulfills both physically and spiritually the prophecy that Japheth would "dwell in the tents of Shem." The middle wall of partition between Jew and Gentile has been eliminated in Christ.

As tenacious and indominable in carrying the Word of God as they ever were in absorbing territory, the "Bear" has been a mighty force in the spread of Christianity. Since the events recorded in the book of Acts, the Church has extended itself world-wide both spiritually and physically. Represented in every nation and even among some governments of the world, the descendants of Japheth have spread their faith to the ends of the earth. Until very recently Christianity was the world's leading religion. And wherever God's Word has been taught, people have profited from His message. As the writer of Proverbs stated:

Proverbs 29:18 Where there is no vision
(*revelation*), the people perish: But
he that keepeth the law (*the Word
of God*), happy is he.

Working among God's people, the Scriptures bring God's blessings to any nation.

But just as Israel, nourished by God for 2000 years, rejected Him and was punished for her unfaithfulness, so the Gentiles after 2000 privileged years as custodians of God's Word have largely rejected that Word and will be judged in turn. God's appeal--to believe the gospel of grace and be saved--is falling on deaf ears, and His requirement--to live according to His standards--is being ignored. As a result of this rejection, the Western world is coming apart at the seams. The things of God have no place today among any but a remnant in all the nations of the world.

In order to solve their economic, social, and political problems, the nations of Europe are slowly relinquishing their sovereignty to form a European Community. This movement will be led more and more by Germany, descendants of Gomer, who see the Aryan race as superior and will seek to form it, as they attempted to do during World War II, into a power that will, economically and militarily
rule the world. With the demise of Javan's influence, after the confrontation with the Ram, other descendants of Japheth, under the leadership of Gomer, will polarize into a constituency which will form the kingdom of the Bear, the second of the "four

notable ones toward the four winds of heaven."[3]

The Third Notable One

The third notable horn is the same kingdom symbolized by the leopard in Daniel 7, and is composed of the descendants of the sons of Ham in the last days. According to Daniel, this spotted leopard "had upon its back four wings of a fowl; and the beast had also four heads" (Daniel 7:6). Spots and/or blemishes are bibical symbols of the contamination of sin. In several passages elsewhere in Scripture the Hebrew word Daniel uses to describe the leopard of his vision is translated "blemish":

Exodus 12:5 Your lamb shall be without blemish.

29:1 and two rams without blemish.

Leviticus 1:3 Let him offer a male without blemish.

Under Mosaic law, spotted or blemished animals, because of their impurity, were unacceptable to God as sacrificial animals. Daniel's spotted leopard represents that which was once pure but which became stained by rebellion against the theocratic rule of God. This rebellion began with Ham's refusal to respect the spiritual position of his father, Noah, God's representative in the post-diluvian world (Genesis 9:20-24). Subsequent biblical history records the antipathy of the descendants of Ham's sons (Cush,

---

[3] For details on the formation of the "Bear" see our book on *The Four Beasts of Daniel 7.*

Mizraim, Phut, and Canaan) toward Israel and the statutes of God, a rebellion most pronounced among the Canaanites.

The leopard which Daniel saw in his vision had two sets of wings of fowl on its back. These wings differ from those of the eagle, whose wings symbolize not only royalty but God's enabling power (Isaiah 40:31). In Scripture fowl are scavengers, birds regarded as unclean and not fit to be used as sacrifice to God. A good example of this symbolism appears in Genesis 15:11 when, in conjunction with God's covenant, Abraham made a sacrifice which the scavengers attempted to destroy to interdict the covenant. Another example appears in Matthew 13:4, in the parable of the sower, where the fowls of the air came and devoured the seed that fell by the way-side. The seed represents the Word of God, and the fowls are again portrayed as willing instruments of destruction, ready to undo God's work in the world.

Originally designed by God to rid the world of dead flesh, fowls, rather than making their own kill, are called upon to devour what is already dead (see Deuteronomy 28:26; I Samuel 17:44-46; Revelation 18:2; 19:17,21). In Deuteronomy 28, the extended passage of curses pronounced upon Israel for disobedience, the fowls represent a warning to the nation.

> Deuteronomy 28:26 And thy carcase shall be meat unto all fowls of the air, and unto the beasts of the earth, and no man shall fray them away.

Noting that the kingdom of the Antichrist has the

body of the leopard (Revelation 13:2) this curse will certainly find its final fulfillment in the "time of Jacob's trouble," the persecution of Israel when, according to Zechariah 13:8, two thirds of the nation will perish and become "meat unto all fowls of the air."

In addition to the wings, there were four heads on the leopard of Daniel's vision in chapter 7. The word "head" denotes rule or authority and these four heads properly represent four separate seats of authority among Ham's descendants. They most likely symbolize the four lines descending from the four sons of Ham: Cush, Mizraim, Phut and Canaan--each of whom has played an important role in the biblical history of Israel. As we explained in our book, *Come Thou Reign Over Us*,

> The spiritual condition of individual members of the lines fades into obscurity, but the divine narrative does record the continuing deterioration of the line of Ham in their relationship to God. It may be seen in each of Ham's sons; Cush, Mizraim, and Phut, but most pronounced in the line of Canaan...The attempts by Satan to destroy God's purpose in Shem, and his use of Cush, Mizraim and Canaan to do so fill the pages of the Old Testament.[6]

In the end time, as Shem and Japheth each unite under a central head, the descendants of Ham will continue to struggle among themselves for power. They will remain divided into four camps until dominated by the Beast (Antichrist) during the Tribulation period. Before moving on to a discussion of "the fourth notable one" we will take up, in sequence, the role of the descendants of each of Ham's sons in God's plan for the last days.

Cush

Of Ham's four sons Cush was evidently the eldest, and while the word "Cush" is usually rendered "Ethiopia" in the Old Testament, this is not a translation but rather an interpretation based upon the belief that Cush's descendants settled primarily in Northeast Africa. According to ISBE:

> The sons of Cush named in Genesis 10:7 (Saba, Havilah, Sabtah, Raamah, and Sabtechah) and the grandsons through Raamah (Sheba and Dedan) who are also mentioned in the same verse, appear to have nearly all settled in areas adjacent to the Persian Gulf. There is some evidence that Sabtechah may have been on the eastern shores of the Persian Gulf; but most of the others were sprinkled about the western shores, around the southern tip of the Arabian Peninsula, even roaming into the interior of the Peninsula (i.e.) the Sabeans, Job 1:15). Some feel there is evidence that at least some of their descendants crossed over into East Africa with other Cushites into not only Ethiopia but present day Somaliland.[7]

In fact, Cush became the "hero god" of Babylon, known as Marduk or Merodach.

> Genesis 10:8 And Cush begat Nimrod: he began to be a mighty one in the earth.

While most commentators credit Nimrod with being

90

the founder of Babylon in Genesis 10:10, the proper name, Nimrod, is a transliteration of the Hebrew word "nimrod," a niphal participle of "*merad*," meaning "rebel," into English and should be translated, "Cush begat rebellion." It was Cush who rebelled against God and founded anti-God kingdoms, one of which was Babylon. As Marduk or *Merodach*, the rebel, he was the instigator of the Babylonian system that will exist until it is destroyed by the Lord Jesus at the Battle of Armageddon. (See first book of this series, *Come Thou Reign Over Us*.)

According to the Babylonian account of creation, Marduk (Cush) also claimed to have created man, thus deifying himself:

> "Blood I shall amass," he confided to Ea, his father; "bone I shall frame, and set up a creature." "Man" shall be his name. Yes , Man! He will be required to serve the gods, and these, then, will be free to repose at ease.[8]

The Bible is not derived from these Sumero-Semitic myths, but rather mythology is often derived from events recorded in the Bible. This creation account is Satan's perversion of God's truth and this perversion is only part of the damage Cush did at the Tower of Babel. After that episode and the scattering of the people, some of his descendants migrated into Africa, where they continued to practice and promulgate their idolatry and rebellion.

In the last days the descendants of Cush will polarize into a power-seeking force throughout the world. The Dallas Morning News reported May 23, 1990 the following from Iyapo Jahi's address commemorating African Liberation Day (emphasis ours):

> African Americans must realize they are part of an international struggle for freedom by blacks around the world, Pan-African leaders in Dallas said Wednesday....Wherever African people are, they're exploited all around the world, said Iyapo Jahi, one of the organizers of African Liberation Day, which will be celebrated Friday and Saturday in Dallas. In Africa, in Europe, in Asia...we've got to understand that in order to change this, we can't just deal with little pockets here and there. We've got to deal with the overall picture, he said. And it's going to be through political education that people will begin to understand this. The Pan-African movement seeks to *unite people* of African descent...As Malcolm X began to realize during his lifetime, Msr. Jahi said, African-Americans must understand that.[9]

As the Morning News also reported, and as the above U.S. celebration confirms, this movement is not new and it is not confined to the blacks of Africa:

> The first Pan-African Conference was held in 1900. From its inception, the Pan-African movement bound Africans in Africa with its people abroad. Marcus Garvey and W.E.B. Dubois in the United States, Kwame Nkrumah in Ghana and Ahmed Seku Ture in Guinea are historic figures in the Pan-African Movement. The first Conference of Independent States was conducted in 1958. The meeting involved African heads of states to organize countries and help countries not yet free. The conference established April 15 as Africa

Freedom Day, but in 1963 the date was changed to May 25 and the celebration was renamed African Liberation Day, said organizer Jahi...Mr. Jahi added, "They won't be free until they have actually achieved Pan-Africanism, *which is the unification of Africa under scientific socialism.*" [10]

This movement toward "black power" is gaining influence in American politics. Nelson Mandela, rebel leader of the African National Congress was recently released from a South African prison where he spent nearly 30 years for murder and inciting armed insurrection. Because of his stand against apartheid, he received a royal reception on his visit to the United States and at the United Nations, which reflects the appeal this push for power is gaining among Americans. But for whatever motivation, whether it be noble or self-seeking, the unification of the people of African descent around the world will represent one of the four heads of the leopard Daniel saw in his vision of the end times.

Mizraim

Another of the four heads of Daniel's leopard is Mizraim, second son of Ham (Genesis 10:13-14) whose descendants settled part of Northeast Africa. While his range was not entirely limited to that country, in Scripture Mizraim is usually translated Egypt. This country, which grew up along the Nile River valley is known as one of the world's earliest and greatest civilizations. At best a weak ally of Israel and at other times an avowed enemy, Egypt has always been an independent entity (See Zechariah 14:18-19). As such, Egypt will not join the coalition of Cushite nations in the rest of Africa. Instead she will probably consolidate an Arabic-speaking bloc of people under her power, organizing them along the lines of the Pan-Arab Union proposed in 1960. In the last days, Egypt will, as she is now, be pressured to accept the imposition of Islamic fundamentalism which will be promoted, not only by the Ram, but later by the Semites under the kingdom symbolized by the lion with eagle's wings. Whether or not she resists that threat remains to be seen but she will, at length, remain independent and another head of the leopard.

Phut

Yet another of the four heads of the leopard Daniel prophesied would appear in the last days is Phut, who, while listed as a son of Ham (Genesis 10:6), does not have his genealogy recorded alongside of Cush, Mizraim, and Canaan in the Table of Nations. We may safely assume, however, that this missing genealogy does not prove that Phut died with no descendants, since he is named among the nations active in the army of Tyre in Ezekiel 27:10.

From the inscriptions of Darius I of Persia (522-486 B.C.), we can identify the land Phut settled as Cyrenaica in North Africa west of Egypt.[11] Interestingly, this area includes Libya, Algeria, Tunisia and Morocco--nations which have formerly played a very minor part in the history of Israel but which have begun to assert themselves in these last days as fervent pockets of Islamic fundamentalism harboring terrorists and enemies of Israel.

Canaan

A final head of the leopard in Daniel's vision

represents Canaan, the youngest son of Ham, whose role in the prophecy of Noah, repeated for emphasis, must therefore not be ignored. Before any of the sons of Shem or Japheth are named in Scripture, Ham's son, Canaan, is mentioned five times (Genesis 9:18,22,25,26,27) and it was Canaan, not Ham who received Noah's curse:

> Genesis 9:25 And he said, Cursed be Canaan; a servant of servants shall he be unto his brethren.

Probably because the Canaanites have exhibited the flawed character of the Hamites more than any of Ham's other descendants, Satan has always been able to use the descendants of Canaan to oppose God's plan for Israel. For example, when Abram first entered the land, he found that the Canaanites had preceded him and had occupied the land that God had promised him.

> Genesis 12:6 And Abram passed through the land unto the place of Sichem, unto the plain of Moreh. And the Canaanite was then in the land.

Having usurped the land designed for God's chosen people, the Canaanites were always a thorn in the side of Israel. Under judgment for their depravity and idolatry, the Canaanites were to be either destroyed or driven out of the land when Israel returned from Egyptian captivity. When Israel failed to carry out God's mandate and allowed the Canaanites to remain in the land, eventually adopting their ways, God instead drove Israel from their land as He had warned in Numbers 33:50-56.

Though Israel has been in dispersion for 2000 years, the remnants of the Canaanite tribes, the "fellahin" (meaning native occupants of the land) remained in the land.

In the late 19th century God began to return the Jews to their land by means of the Zionist movement. In 1948, after the holocaust of World War II, that movement was augmented by the rebirth of the state of Israel. At that time Palestine was a part of Jordan, and the Palestinians fought unsuccessfully alongside the Arabs to expel Israel. During the 1967 war with the Arab states, Israel occupied East Jerusalem and the West Bank (claimed by Jordan), the Golan Heights (claimed by Syria), Gaza and the Sinai Peninsula (claimed by Egypt). The Palestinians on the West Bank and those who left as refugees formed the Palestinian Liberation Organization (PLO) to drive Israel out of the Middle East. The Palestinians, descended from the original Canaanite tribes, are to this present day still a thorn in the side of Israel.

We should note that in referring to the kingdom of the leopard, Daniel observed that "dominion was given to it" (Daniel 7:6). Scripture does not tell us that dominion was given to the lion and the bear. The right to rule was given to both Shem and Japheth when Noah blessed them (Genesis 9:26-27), but Ham's descendants have, to a large extent, been under the rule of either Shem or Japheth ever since. The ancient world powers, Babylon, Medo-Persia, Rome; later the Byzantine, Mohammedan, and Ottoman empires all extended their control into the territory of Ham. Later, European colonialism invaded the interior of Africa and only in our lifetime has the control of Shem and Japheth over the descendants of Ham diminished as the rise of the leopard is taking place.

The Fourth Notable One

The fourth "notable one" of Daniel 8:8 that "came up toward the four winds of heaven" refers to the same kingdom symbolized in Daniel 7:7 by the beast that is "diverse from them all." Defying description, this fourth "notable one," described only as a "fourth beast, diverse from all that were before it," will originate from Israel in the last days.

Having been taught for years that Daniel's "diverse beast" will be a revived Roman Empire which may also be identified with "the iron legs, with feet part of iron and part of clay" of the image in Daniel 2, some of our readers will no doubt find it difficult to alter their thinking on the matter. Walvoord has rightly observed that:

> The crucial issue in the interpretation of the entire book of Daniel, and especially of chapter 7, is the identification of the fourth beast...Conservative scholars with few exceptions generally identify the fourth beast as Rome.[12]

Because the identification of the fourth beast is so crucial to an understanding of all Bible prophecy, we would urge the student of prophecy to concentrate on what the Bible teaches, putting aside for the moment the traditional view in order to take a fresh look at this fourth kingdom.

It is in this last beast that the four visions of the book of Daniel intersect: (1) the legs of iron and the feet of iron mixed with clay of Nebuchadnezzar's image dream in Daniel 2; (2) the fourth or "diverse beast" in Daniel 7, (3) the fourth "notable one" in Daniel 8; (4) and the king of the north in Daniel 11:21. Symbolizing a kingdom that is well equipped for war, this "diverse beast" is dreadful and terrible with great iron teeth which devour, and hooves of bronze (7:19) to break in pieces and stamp all that oppose him (7:7).

In each of the former books of this series we stressed the fact that the kingdom of the Antichrist will originate in Israel. Specifically, it will begin with the northern kingdom of Israel and will expand to embrace not only the southern kingdom but the entire world. A nation set apart, "diverse" from all other nations, Israel was chosen for God's service; but, at the end, it will be a thoroughly corrupted version of God's original purpose and the willing tool of Satan. Since we cannot restate here all the biblical proof we have set forth in our previous books on the subject of Israel's role in the end times, and since ours is a completely new eschatological system, we can only suggest that our readers avail themselves of these books in order to see for themselves what the Scriptures have to say on the subject.

The era when this final kingdom rules will be characterized by extremes of sin: people will be exceedingly wicked, violent, hateful, vindictive, cruel, and deceitful; the kingdom's climax will occur during the "last days" Paul described to Timothy:

II Timothy 3:1 This know also, that in the last days perilous times shall come.

2 For men shall be lovers of their own selves, covetous, boasters,

proud, blasphemers, disobedient to parents, unthankful, unholy,

3 Without natural affection, trucebreakers, false accusers, incontinent, fierce, despisers of those that are good,

4 Traitors, heady, highminded, lovers of pleasure more than lovers of God:

5 Having a form of godliness, but denying the power thereof: from such turn away.

During this time, persecution of those who believe God's Word, who attempt to practice God's will and live according to His standards will be at its height, often resulting in martyrdom.

Today Israel is divided politically, culturally, and religiously. The Labor Party wants to trade land for peace. The Likud Party resists the notion of restoring to the Palestinians the land conquered in the 1967 war and favors the establishment of Jewish settlements on the occupied West Bank. We may expect a division of Israel into two states again, especially in light of Ezekiel's prophecy that only the Son of David will be able to bring both Judah and Ephraim together permanently (Ezekiel 37:16-28). The northern state of Israel will then be positioned to become the "diverse beast" of Daniel 7 (specific details of these climatic events in the history of Israel are seen in Daniel 11, beginning in verse 5). The southern kingdom will attack the northern kingdom with some initial success, but in the end "he shall not be strengthened by it [this struggle] (Daniel 11:7). The king of the north will increase in power and territory until "he shall stand in the glorious land, which by his hand shall be consumed" (Daniel 11:16). Yet his reign will be short-lived: "He shall stumble and fall, and not be found" (Daniel 11:19). After a temporary leader arises, who himself will rule but a very short time (Daniel 11:20), a "vile person" will finally take command (Daniel 11:21). He is the "little horn" of Daniel 7:8 and 8:9, and "the beast out of the sea" (the Antichrist) of Revelation 13:1. From Daniel 11:21 to the end of the book we have a detailed account of Israel's suffering ("the time of Jacob's trouble") at the hands of their pseudo "messiah."

Under the rule of these four kingdoms (the four "notable ones"), the world will be plunged into economic chaos. Three of the kingdoms, recognizing their hopeless condition, will seek for someone to provide the solution and the "little horn" will present himself as the Messiah of Israel and the world. The descendants of Shem, Ham and Japheth will surrender their autonomy to become part of the kingdom of the "little horn" and that world-wide kingdom will take on the configuration seen in Revelation 13:2 with the body of a leopard, the feet of a bear, and the mouth of a lion.

Each of the three races is polarizing even now to promote their own ends as each increasingly realizes that they have never prospered in conjunction with one of the others. While Islamic Fundamentalism is uniting the forces of Shem, Germany is drawing the descendants of Japheth into an Economic Community that will eventually include all nations of the western coalition, along with countries of Asia, Australia and New Zealand. Nations of the third world, too, are uniting. The descendants of Cush are bringing the nations of Africa together and attracting blacks from the rest of the world. Mizraim (Egypt) is resisting the push of the Islamic Fundamentalists but will probably form a coalition of moderate Arabs. The Palestinians (Canaan) while speaking Arabic and clamoring for help on this basis find themselves more and more isolated. They are forming into a state without territory, but we predict that Jordan will, upon the death of the present ruler, become a Palestinian state. Jordan is already 60% Palestinian.

Israel remains a people separate from all the nations. No nation in the world wants to join with them in their struggle to become a nation recognized and respected by the rest of the world. Even the United States, their most supportive ally since Israel became a nation again, is distancing itself in order to appear even-handed to Arab interests. Although the Palestinian issue of "land for peace" will probably be the catalyst to divide the nation of Israel, they have long been divided culturally and religiously. But as the Palestinian issue recedes into the territory east of the Jordan, both states will begin to prosper economically. That ability to remain financially strong in the face of world economic chaos will, in the end time, draw all nations of the earth to put their trust in the "little horn."

End Notes

1. Keil and Delitzsch, pages 222-223
2. Pentecost, page 437
3. Hatti, page 4

4. Wallbank, Taylor, Bailkey, page 174
5. Time Magazine, May 24, 1990
6. Matheny, Come Thou Reign Over Us, page 26
7. ISBE, Vol. II, page 1345; Vol. IV, pp 2520, 2636, 2752, 2753
8. Ibid, page 84
9. Dallas Morning News, May 24, 1990, page 10
10. Ibid, Page 10
11. Unger, page 53
12. Walvoord, Daniel, page 159

Chapter 5

The Little Horn

Daniel 8:9 And out of one of them came forth a little horn.

The clause above literally reads: "And out of them came forth a horn of one, insignificant." Thus from the four "notable ones," or horns (identified as the four "beasts out of the sea" in Daniel 7) arises an authority who will play the dominant role in world events during the final days. Throughout history, one nation has always led the world as the imperial power. In the end-time, Israel will become that dominant force. Frequently, the ruler of the leading nation comes into power by force of arms, but the "little horn" will devise a most successful method of his own to win universal authority over mankind. We find the details of his strategy outlined in both Daniel 8:25 and Daniel 11:21-23 (emphasis ours):

Daniel 8:25 And through his policy also he shall cause craft to prosper in his hand: and he shall magnify himself in his heart, and *by peace shall destroy many...*

11:21 And in his estate shall stand up a vile person, to whom they shall not give the honour of the kingdom: but he shall come in *peaceably, and obtain the kingdom by flatteries.*

23 And after the league made with him he shall work *deceitfully*: for he shall come up, and shall become strong with a small people.

Initially the "little horn" will gain control of the "diverse beast" through a coalition of the ten northern tribes (the ten horns): later he will maintain that control with an iron fist. Having consolidated his position in the northern kingdom, with the clear support of the ten northern tribes, the "little horn" will turn his attention first to the southern kingdom and then to the centers of power among Shem, Ham, and Japheth.

While the concept of an Israel with the power to impose its will on the rest of the world may seem remote at this point in history, with the demise of the worldwide influence first of the Ram and then of the Goat nations, Israel stands to become the foremost military power in the world. While the states of the old Soviet Union are dismantling their nuclear warheads, and the United States and other Western powers are systematically reducing their nuclear capability, Israel will not even admit to possessing the atomic bomb, permitting no inspection teams to enter the nation. When the rest of the world is effectively disarmed, Israel, with their nuclear potential intact, will have no difficulty imposing their form of "peace" on the whole world.

The Traditional View Of The "Little Horn"

Most conservative commentators identify the "little horn" of Daniel 8 with Antiochus Epiphanes, eighth king in the Syrian dynasty of the Seleucid kingdom, who reigned from 175-164 B.C. Keil summarizes the sources for the traditional view as follows:

> The one of the four horns from which the little horn grew up is the Syrian monarchy, and the horn growing up out of it is the king Antiochus Epiphanes, as Josephus (Ant. x.11.7) and all interpreters acknowledge, on the ground of I Macc. i.10.[1]

We must make an important point immediately with regard to the sources Keil relies upon to support this interpretation: both are *extra-biblical*. A Jewish historian who defected to the Romans during the campaign against Judaea by the armies of Vespasian shortly before the destruction of Jerusalem in A.D. 70, Josephus composed a fascinating secular history, albeit somewhat slanted to suit both his Roman captors and his Jewish heritage. As Whiston explains in the following (emphasis ours):

> Flavius Josephus (A.D. 37-c.100) is the author of what has become for Christianity perhaps the most significant *extra-biblical writing* of the first century. His works are the principal source for the history of the Jews from the reign of Antiochus Epiphanes (B.C. 175-164) to the fall of Masada in A.D. 73, and therefore, are of incomparable value for determining the *setting* of late inter-testamental and New Testament times.[2]

The second source Keil lists to support the traditional interpretation of the "little horn," the books of the Maccabees, come from the Apocrypha and are not accepted as canonical in either the Hebrew or Protestant tradition as noted below (emphasis ours):

The Apocrypha is the name given to 14 books which originated in the period between the OT and the NT after the OT canon had closed...These apocryphal books were never in the OT Hebrew canon. They were included in the Septuagint and the Latin Vulgate, being placed between the OT and NT. The Roman Catholic church receives 11 of the 14 as so-called "deutero-canonical" books, declaring them a part of Scripture by the Council of Trent in A.D. 1546. *Protestants deny the canonical status of these books* on the basis of both internal and external evidence. They were never recognized as Scripture by the Jews, nor by Jesus, nor by the NT, nor by any of the Church Fathers who objectively examined the evidence.[3]

Because they are not part of Scripture these books cannot supply our ultimate source for truth. With the Bible as our sole authority, it is not wise to rely on any extra-biblical source for the interpretation of Daniel; such sources may help us identify the setting of, and perhaps even provide some important historical data about the events in the Old Testament, but they are *not* acceptable bases for interpretation. We must also remind our readers that another proponent of the interpretation which placed Antiochus Epiphanes in Scripture was the pagan philosopher, Porphyry, who held that the book of Daniel was written about 150 B.C. and was thus not a prophecy but a forgery, a history of intertestamental times. Claiming that the events of Daniel fit perfectly with the history of the intertestamental period,

Porphyry used Daniel's prophecy to support his own interpretation of that period. In this manner he sought to discredit Daniel as a prophet and the book as a divine message from God to His people, Israel.

While vociferously defending Daniel as a legitimate prophet, Jerome (a Christian scholar of the fourth century A.D.), nevertheless incorporated Porphyry's intertestamental argument into his commentary on Daniel; and, as we have noted earlier in our works on Daniel, no substantive change in this interpretation has occurred in 1500 years. The determination that the "little horn" of Daniel 8 was Antiochus Epiphanes, a king of Syria depends for its validity on three invalid sources: an Apocryphal book (I Maccabees); Josephus, a secular Jewish historian; and Porphyry, a pagan philosopher.

Even when relying on the above three sources Walvoord recognizes a wide difference of opinion among commentators on the interpretation of the "little horn" of Daniel 8:

> Although a great deal of variation is found in details of interpretation, four major views emerge: 1) the historical view that all of Daniel 8 has been fulfilled; (2) the futuristic view, the idea that it is entirely future; (3) the view based upon the principle of dual fulfillment of prophecy, that Daniel 8 is intentionally a prophetic reference both to Antiochus Epiphanes, now fulfilled, and to the end of the age and final world ruler who persecutes Israel before the second advent; (4) the view that the passage is prophecy, historically fulfilled but intentionally typical of similar events and

We firmly hold that number 2 above is the correct position to hold on Daniel's prophecy. Yet although the passage presents every indication that all the events recorded in Daniel 8 will occur in the end time, the traditional view has become firmly entrenched. But support for a dual fulfillment involving Antiochus Epiphanes could only be held to be true if he were mentioned in the Bible. To reach into secular history covering a period of several hundred years and randomly choose events to make a scenario fit the Bible, and, further, to do so on the authority of Porphyry (a pagan) is irresponsible. We reiterate that the Bible is its own best interpreter and that Antiochus Epiphanes is not mentioned in the Bible. He, like Alexander the Great, lived during the intertestamental period when God was silent to Israel. Thus he qualifies no more as an antitype of the "little horn" than do other secular leaders who have persecuted the Jews, and there have been many. The principal reason for the identification of Antiochus with Daniel's "little horn" is that in the time of both Porphyry and Jerome, the Jews were--justifiably--as involved emotionally with the Maccabean era and the history of Josephus as they have been in this century with their persecution under Hitler's Third Reich. Nevertheless, neither the books of the Maccabees nor the works of Josephus are a part of Scripture; nor do they deserve to be endorsed on that divine level.

If we depend only on Scripture for our interpretation, we see that the "little horn" of both Daniel 7 and Daniel 8 is God's designation for the "insignificant authority" ("little" meaning insignificant and "horn" indicating authority) who will come into power as the head of the "diverse beast" in the last days. He will have total control of the world for 42 months (Daniel 7:25; Revelation 13:5). To counter the use of extra-biblical sources for aid in our interpretation we need only turn to the Old Testament for more apt representations of the "little horn."

Recorded in Judges 9, the Parable of the Trees illustrates to Israel the kind of king they will eventually embrace and the threat he will be to them. The Jews of the Old Testament always demanded but were rarely able to interpret (much less abide by), the signs given them. Thus, rather than a blessing, the "little horn" will present a real danger to Israel, when we interpret their future behavior according to what a summary of Judges 9 demonstrates:

In defiance of God's law, the men of Shechem made Abimelech, the illegitimate son of Gideon by a Canaanite woman, king over them. Jotham, Gideon's youngest son, and the only one to survive the slaughter of his house by Abimelech, stood on the top of Mt. Gerizim and cried out against the injustice of Abimelech. Jotham related the following parable to the people below to describe the person they had chosen to be their king: The trees went forth to anoint a king over them, offering the kingship to the olive tree, the fig tree, and the vine (all legitimate symbols of the nation). When all these refused to leave their God-given vocation to be king, the trees offered the crown to the bramble (thistle or thorn). After accepting the kingship, this insignificant bush, with no earthly value other than to be a source of pain, threatened the nation of trees with the fire of destruction if they did not give him their total allegiance.[1]

The bramble, not Antiochus Epiphanes, is a scriptural type of the "little horn." Like the bramble, he will be a thorn in the side of God's people, causing them pain and destruction. And, like the bramble, he will be so insignificant that his name is not even memorialized in Scripture, except by a title, the "beast" (Revelation 13:1). Yet in spite of his unworthiness, the "little horn" will be accepted, first by the majority of Israel to become the leader of their nation, and then by the world to lead Satan's system to oppose God and His faithful remnant. In the gospel of John, Jesus predicted that Israel would embrace just such an insignificant leader:

> John 5:43 I am come in my Father's name, and ye receive me not: if another shall come in his own name, him ye will receive.

The "little horn" will be the lowest of the low, and his dominion will reflect both his own depravity and the spiritual condition of those he rules. The earthly "name" he will espouse remains to be seen.

Which Waxed Exceeding Great Toward The South

As we noted in our other books on Daniel, the "little horn," according to the pattern for illegitimate rulers in Scripture, will arise in the northern kingdom

---

[1] For more on this scriptural analogy of the thorn motif in the Old Testament, see the first book of this series, *Come Thou Reign Over Us*.

110

of Israel, probably somewhere in or around the old city of Shechem. (For a detailed explanation of this point, see the first book of this series, *Come Thou Reign Over Us*.) Old Shechem is today the city of Nablus on the West Bank, occupied at present by the armed forces of Israel because it is the center of unrest among the Palestinian population.

The son of a Jewish father by a Canaanite woman, the "little horn" will first attempt to expand his rule to absorb the southern kingdom. Meeting with considerable resistance from that quarter, he will withdraw temporarily, but the defeat of the south, with all that it symbolizes to Israel, will remain his major objective. He will return again but only achieve his goal after a series of campaigns which are detailed in Daniel 11:25-41.

Toward The East

Having failed to conquer the southern kingdom of Israel, the next phrase of this verse tells us the "little horn" will seek to expand his kingdom "toward the East." The book of Numbers identifies the area east of the Jordan River as the land where Reuben, Gad, and half of the tribe of Manasseh were given their inheritance:

Numbers 34:13 And Moses commanded the children of Israel saying, This is the land which ye shall inherit by lot, which the Lord commanded to give unto the nine tribes, and to the half tribe:

14 For the tribe of the children of

Reuben according to the house of their fathers, and the tribe of the children of Gad according to the house of their fathers, have received their inheritance; and half the tribe of Manasseh have received their inheritance.

15 The two tribes and the half tribe have received their inheritance on this side Jordan near Jericho eastward, toward the sunrising.

Today this territory is occupied by the nation of Jordan, a relatively powerless nation whose population is more than 60% Palestinian. Please recall our stipulation that the "diverse beast" of Daniel 7 is the same as the iron kingdom of Daniel 2. When the "little horn" gains control over the iron kingdom described in Daniel 2, he will begin to incorporate the clay of the Canaanites (Palestinians) into the iron in the kingdom of Israel. These Canaanites (Palestinians) will join forces with the "little horn," becoming a part of his kingdom which will at that point begin to deteriorate in every conceivable way. (The biblical evidence for this interpretation is available in the second book of this series, *Gold, Silver, Brass, Iron: Rethinking the Kingdoms of Daniel 2.*)

We have previously demonstrated that all the Semites will polarize into a single kingdom (symbolized by the lion with eagle's wings of Daniel 7) and will become one of the four "notable ones" in the world of the end times. During the reign of the "little horn," the northern kingdom will consolidate under his power *all these Semites*, who are primarily located east of Israel. This group will include descendants of Shem: Elam, Asshur, Aram, and Arphaxad (both Isaac and Ishmael); descendants of Esau (Edom); descendants of Lot (Moab and Ammon); and all of the descendants of Abraham by Keturah (see Genesis 25:1-4). All of this wealth and territory, along with that of Jordan's Palestinians, will come under the control of the "little horn" in the east.

Toward The Pleasant Land

The word *land* in verse 9 in the KJV is italicized indicating that it does not appear in the original language. Apparently the translators added this word to give sense to the above phrase, because the Hebrew word translated "pleasant" is a term often used to describe the land of Israel (Jer. 3:19; Eze. 20:6, 15; 26:20; Daniel 11:16, 41, 45). This Hebrew word "tsebiy" can be translated "pleasant" to indicate prominence; "splendor (as conspicuous); also a gazelle (as beautiful): - beautiful (-ty), glorious (-ry); goodly, pleasant, roe (buck)."[5] Used in this context, the word "tsebiy" suggests that the "little horn" will wage a campaign against all that is pleasant, beautiful, glorious, or splendid in Israel. A destroyer rather than a builder, he will--after conquering much that originally belonged to Israel--launch a campaign consolidating his power in the world. A ruthless dictator, he will eliminate all opposition to his authority by requiring that every individual wear his mark of allegiance under threat of starvation or execution (Revelation 13:15-17).

The Hebrew word "el," translated "toward" in the above phrase, is a prime particle properly denoting motion toward.[6] Where the motion or direction implied appears from the context to be of a hostile character, "el" signifies *against.*[7] Since the "little horn" will be moving to conquer, we may assume that his movements will be hostile. Therefore the entire phrase could read, "*against the south, against the east, against that which is pleasant, goodly, beautiful, or glorious.*"

And It Waxed Great, Even To The Host Of Heaven

We come now to one of the more intriguing passages in the entire book of Daniel. While many commentators recognize the difficulties involved in translating verses 11 and 12, we can overcome those problems by considering these two verses in their full context, beginning in verse 10 and continuing through verse 14. Had the reading of this passage not been invested with the traditional interpretation, that verses 3-8 refer to Alexander the Great and that verses 9-10 refer to Antiochus Epiphanes, it might well have been seen in its true light long before now.

The Hebrew word, "gadol," which the KJV translates "waxed great" in this passage is a stative verb, one which indicates a state of being great, rather than a condition of becoming (waxing, or growing) great. Since no Hebrew term which can properly be translated "waxed" appears here, we can be sure that at this point in Daniel's narrative the "little horn" is not in the process of becoming great, but already is great. And because the verb "gadol" is in the imperfect tense which loosely approximates the future tense in English), a more accurate translation of the entire phrase should read, "and he shall be great, even to the host of heaven."

The phrase translated "even to" in this passage comes from the Hebrew word "ad," "(used as a prep., adv. or conj.: especially with a prep.); as far (long, or much) as, whether of space (even unto) or time (during, while, until) or degree (*equally with*)".[8] Although "even to" accurately conveys the sense of the phrase, we prefer the translation emphasized above, "equally with," to suggest that the "little horn" is great "equally with" or "even to" the host of heaven. At this point in the text we can begin to understand the context of verses 10-14. This entire passage of Daniel deals with the power of the "little horn" in contrast to that of the "host of heaven." If we keep that context in mind as we proceed through the passage, its content will become clear. Read in this light, the passage alludes to no "daily sacrifice," nor does it refer to the defilement of the Temple in the days of Antiochus Epiphanes. Instead, we find here the Old Testament counterpart to the "war in heaven" passage of Revelation 12. It is here that Satan enters into the "little horn" and manifests his power to engage a third part of the former angelic host with him in his rebellion.

The "little horn", now empowered by Satan, will have at his disposal all the demonic principalities and powers who exercise their spiritual wickedness in the heavenlies (Ephesians 6:12). Remembering that Satan's ambition throughout history has been to rise above God and control all of His creation, we see in this passage an outline of the battle lines for Satan's attempt to wrest that control from the host of heaven. In the last days the "little horn's" power will be great *equally with* (even to) the host of heaven, and Satan will stand ready to implement the purpose he stated in the famous five "I wills" of Isaiah 14 (emphasis ours):

Isaiah 14:12 How art thou fallen from heaven, O Lucifer, son of the morning! how art thou cut down to the ground, which didst weaken the nations!

13 For thou hast said in thine heart, *I will ascend into heaven, I will exalt my throne above the stars of God: I will sit also upon the mount of the congregation, in the sides of the north:*

14 *I will ascend above the heights of the clouds; I will be like the most High.*

We are being shown the impending confrontation: Satan's ancient desire to contend for the right to supercede God; his demon hosts aligned against the angelic hosts. If we are to understand fully these verses of Daniel, we should review the entire companion passage in Revelation 12 (condensed below) and note the similarities (emphasis ours).

Revelation 12:3 And there appeared another wonder in heaven; and, behold, a great red dragon, having *seven heads and ten horns and seven crowns upon his heads.*

4 *And his tail drew the third part of the stars of heaven and did cast them to the earth;* and the dragon stood before the woman who was ready to be delivered, to devour her child as soon as it was born.

7 *And there was war in heaven;*
  Michael and his angels fought
  against the dragon and the dragon
  fought and his angels,

8 And prevailed not, neither was
  their place found any more in
  heaven.

9 *And the great dragon was cast out,*
  that old serpent, called the Devil,
  and Satan, which deceiveth the
  whole world: *he was cast out into*
  the earth, and his angels were
  cast out with him.

12 Therefore rejoice, ye heavens, and
  ye that dwell in them. Woe to
  the inhabiters of the earth and of
  the sea! *for the devil is come down*
  unto you, having great wrath,
  because he knoweth that he hath but
  a short time.

Revelation 12:3 portrays Satan possessed of seven heads, ten horns, and seven crowns whose power he will impart to the "little horn" during the final 42 months (3 1/2 years) of this age. Revelation 12 is a parenthetic chapter whose purpose is to introduce certain personages active in this ultimate confrontation: Satan, Israel, Christ, demonic hosts, the angelic hosts, and Michael (the prince of the angelic hosts) and those myriads of believers, both Jew and Gentile, who have hazarded their lives for the Word of God.

And Cast Down Of The Host And Of The Stars To The Ground And Stamped Upon Them

The KJV provides a good translation of the rest of Daniel 8:10 except for the italicized word "some," which does not appear in the original. Literally the passage reads, "And cast down to earth from the host and from the stars and trampled (or stamped) them." The word translated "trampled" here is the same used in 8:7 to describe the Goat's casting the Ram to the ground and "stamping" upon him. To avoid imposing personal presuppositions on the text, it is always best to follow the normal sequence of the Hebrew. The above passage is not difficult in the Hebrew, and by keeping to the original rather than interpolating extra words into the text we see that it still speaks of the struggle between the host of heaven and the "little horn" invested with Satan's power. Some hint of this power is also suggested in Revelation 13:12-14.

As we mentioned earlier, commentators generally agree that Daniel 8:11-12 are very difficult to interpret. Walvoord confirms that:

> Up to Daniel 8:11, it is not difficult to find fulfillment of the vision in the history of the Medo-Persian, Alexandrian, and post-Alexandrian periods. Beginning with verse 11, however, expositors have differed widely as to whether the main import of the passage refers to Antiochus Epiphanes, with complete fulfillment in his lifetime, or whether the passage either primarily or secondarily refers also to the end of the age, that is, the period of great tribulation preceding the second coming

of Jesus Christ. The divergence of interpretation is so wide as to be confusing to the student of Daniel. As Montgomery states, verse 11 and 12 "constitute...the most difficult short passage of the bk.[9]

Walvoord's quote explains the confusion that has resulted because of the very problems we have explored elsewhere in this work. By examining Daniel's words carefully and by comparing their usage in these verses to their usage in other passages we hope to reach clearer conclusions than have commentators in the past. The traditional translation of verse 11 is as follows:

> Daniel 8:11 Yea, he magnified himself even to the prince of the host, and by him the daily sacrifice was taken away, and the place of his sanctuary was cast down.

Yea, He Magnified Himself Even To The Prince Of The Host.

To those who are used to reading the above version of the text, its errors may not seem apparent. Yet translators have mangled this clause. To begin, the word "yea" does not appear in the original, nor the italicized word, "himself" which the translators inserted for clarity and which ironically has only added to the confusion surrounding the proper interpretation of the clause.

The word "host" is translated similarly in both the RSV and the ASV from the Hebrew word "tse'ba'ah", which means armies, hosts. (ASV uses "hosts" more often, while RSV uses "army," "service," "company," and for Lord of hosts, ASV uses "Jehovah of hosts", while the NIV uses "Lord Almighty").[10]

The word "magnified" is incorrectly translated from the hiphal stem (causative) of the Hebrew word "gadol." The text does not tell us that the "little horn" magnified himself, but that he was "caused to be great." He derives his power not from himself, but from Satan, who is responsible for his greatness. Let us remember that God's word has already declared the "little horn" an "insignificant authority."

In light of these necessary corrections in translation, the first clause of verse 11 should literally read, "and even to the Prince of the host he is caused to be great". Thus we see that the text is still speaking of the power of the "little horn." "Until" or "even to" the level of the Prince of the host, the "little horn" is caused to be great. This translation correlates with Revelation 12:7-9, which describes Satan's confrontation with Michael, the Prince of the host.

And By Him The Daily Sacrifice Was Taken Away.

Before we begin our exposition of this section, we should note that italics used in printing the word "sacrifice" in verses 11,12, and 13 in the KJV indicate that the word was added to the text of all three verses for clarification and is not present in the Hebrew manuscripts. In this case, as in many other passages, such interpolations are based upon presuppositions which have only confused the passage. Since we are not speaking here of the "daily sacrifices," we have chosen to replace the translation "daily" with normal synonyms like "continual, perpetual", etc., in order to convey the proper meaning.

To begin the exposition of this part of verse 11, the introductory phrase expressed by the Hebrew word "mimenu" should properly be translated "from him," rather than "by him." Hebrew grammar allows "mimenu" to be translated "from him" or "from us" according to the context in which it appears.[11] Since the "little horn" is the central figure in the context of the passage we will translate the word "from him."

What follows "mimenu" in the Hebrew text is the word "rum" meaning height or haughtiness. According to HAW (emphasis ours):

> Three broad groups of ideas are present in non-cultic usages of "rum" and its derivatives: 1) literal height, 2) height as symbolic of positive notions such as glory and exaltation, 3) *height as symbolic of negative notions such as arrogance and pride...*[12]

In the context of our passage (the "little horn's" power), the third usage provides the best translation. HAW enlarges on the negative notions of the word "rum":

> Negative idioms are the following: the high hearted represents presumption (Deut 8:14) or pride (Ezk 31:10). Lofty eyes (Psa 131:1) and the high arm (Job 38:15) are also presumptuous. The "high ones" or the haughty (II Sam 22:28) is a poetic term for the wicked just as terms such as "afflicted" and "humble" describe the righteous.[13]

121

We are now developing the sense of the passage. Rather than some reference to the daily sacrifices in the nation of Israel, the emphasis is still on the person of the "little horn"--an apt description of his presumptive and haughty wickedness. The last word in this section is the Hebrew "tamiyd," which derives from an unused root meaning "to stretch; prop. continuance (as indef. extension); but used only (attributively as adj.) constant (or adv. constantly)... alway (s), continual (employment, ly), ([n]) ever(-more), perpetual."[14] With this definition in mind, we should more accurately translate the phrase, "and from him (the "little horn") haughtiness (arrogance) perpetually (continually)." Emanating from the "little horn" is a constantly haughty self-concept, an attitude which manifests itself by opposing all that is sacred. (The word "tamiyd" is reiterated in Daniel 11:36, where the text, in giving more detail concerning the actions of the "little horn," is properly translated "exalt," as in the clause "he shall exalt himself.")

The Place Of His Sanctuary Was Cast Down.

Moving on to the last clause of verse 11, we find the Hebrew word "makown" translated "place" in this passage is used here denoting "that which is set up," a sacred place where God has established His name; the word "sanctuary" is translated from the Hebrew word "miqdash" meaning holy place, sanctuary, chapel, or hallowed part. As HAW explains:

> The noun "miqdash" is used most frequently in the OT as the designation of the tabernacle and the temple. It is frequently translated "sanctuary" in these cases. In keeping with the basic meaning of the word group that it

represents (qdsh), "miqdash" denotes that which has been devoted to the sphere of the sacred. When it refers to the sanctuary, it connotes the physical area devoted to the worship of God. This area was sacred because it was the place where God dwelled among the people (Ex 25:8) and its sanctity was not to be profaned (lev 12:4; 19:30; 20:3; 21:12;, 23).[15]

Taken all together, this Hebrew phrase should literally read, "and shall be cast down from his holy place". The phrase foretells the same end result recorded in Revelation 12:7-9 (emphasis ours):

Revelation 12:7   And there was war in heaven: Michael and his angels fought against the dragon; and the dragon fought and his angels,

8   And prevailed not; "*neither was their place found any more in heaven.*

9   And the great dragon was *cast out*, that old serpent, called the Devil and Satan, who deceiveth the whole world; *he was cast out into the earth, and his angels were cast out with him.*

Believers have long realized that, according to the Word, Satan still has access to the throneroom of heaven, if only as the "accuser of the brethren" (Job 1:6-12; Revelation 12:10). That exalted privilege will end with the defeat and destruction of his final masterpiece, the "little horn," the "insignificant horn" whose power comes only through Satan's demonic possession. Ezekiel 28 likewise records this ultimate demise of the enemy of both God and man (emphasis ours):

> Ezekiel 28:14 Thou art the anointed cherub that covereth, and I have set thee so; thou wast upon the holy mountain of God; thou hast walked up and down in the midst of the stones of fire.
>
> 15 Thou wast perfect in thy ways from the day that thou wast created, till iniquity was found in thee.
>
> 16 By the multitude of thy merchandise they have filled the midst of thee with violence, and thou hast sinned; therefore, I will cast thee *as profane out of the mountain of God*, and I will destroy thee, O covering cherub, from the midst of the stones of fire.
>
> 17 Thine heart was lifted up because of thy beauty; thou hast corrupted thy wisdom by reason of thy brightness; *I will cast thee to the ground*, I will lay thee before kings, that they may behold thee.

Although Satan's rebellion was judged at the Cross, he has been operating "on appeal" since the time of his initial rebellion in heaven. The protracted period during which God has permitted him to present his case will run out with the defeat of the "little horn."

An Host Was Given Him Against The Daily Sacrifice By Reason Of Transgression.

In its proper context, Daniel 8:12 continues an account of the brief exploits of the "little horn".

> Daniel 8:12   And an host was given him against the daily sacrifice by reason of transgression, and it cast down the truth to the ground; and it practised, and prospered.

As before, we must again eliminate the word "sacrifice" from the translation, following the normal sequence of the Hebrew rather than reading into it personal presuppositions. Corrected, this first clause of verse 12 should properly read: "And an host was given to them to transgress (rebel) continually". This passage refers to the time spoken of in Daniel 11:23, when "the transgressors are come to the full," and in Daniel 11:30-32, where those who do wickedly against the covenant will be corrupted by the "little horn's" flatteries. In contrast to the "host of heaven", this host- -composed of Jew, Gentile, and fallen angels--will have given their allegiance to the "little horn" and will be bent continually on rebellion and transgression. This passage also continues the correlation with Revelation 12, especially verses 12, 13,17.

And It Cast Down The Truth To The Ground; And It Practised, And Prospered.

This is a good translation of the last half of verse 12, with "truth" translated from the Hebrew word "emet," which can also denote faithfulness, verity, fidelity, and firmness. This term is used to describe the Word of God (Psa. 119:142, 151, 160; Dan 10:21; John 17:17), because as HAW states:

> As we study its various contexts, it becomes manifestly clear that there is no truth in the biblical sense, i.e. valid truth, outside God. All truth comes from God and is truth because it is related to God.[16]

The implication of verse 12, then, is that the Word of God, from which all other truth emanates, will be ground into the dust when the "little horn" rules: "The truth was cast to the ground." While both the "little horn" and the host who follow him will deride, reject, and scorn the Word of God, they will nevertheless prosper in all they do for a time.

While the next two words "practiced and prospered" appear in that order in the KJV, they are actually reversed in the original Hebrew. We will therefore consider them in that order in our explanation.

"Prosper" is the Hebrew "tsalach," a prime root which means "to push forward, in various senses (lit. or fig., trans. or intrans.): break out, come (mightily) go over, be good, be meet, be profitable, (cause to, effect, make to, send) prosper (ity, - ous, -ously)."[17] HAW explains the biblical meaning of the word as follows:

> Although true prosperity comes only from

God's blessing, externally it often appears that the wicked prosper... In the last days those who are opposed to God shall prosper for a time through cunning and deceit (Daniel 12ff, 24). But their success will be only temporary, for God is preparing a time of judgment against all evil to accomplish his indignation (Dan 11:36).[18]

The "little horn's" prosperity, his *push forward*, will be great but short-lived, as the prophet repeats in Daniel 11:36:

> Daniel 11:36 And the king shall do according to his will; and he shall exalt himself, and magnify himself above every god, and shall speak marvelous things against the God of gods, and shall *prosper* till the indignation be accomplished; for that which is determined shall be done.

The final word, "practice," in verse 12 is translated from the Hebrew "asah," a prime root meaning "to do or make, in the broadest sense and widest application..."[19] The "little horn" will have unlimited control worldwide with all the resources available to him from Satan's domain. There is a contrast inferred here before both men and angels, of an earth ruled by God or of an earth governed by the norms and standards of hell. But there is no mistaking the implication of the word "practice." The "little horn" will *do* just as he pleases until the time of God's judgment.

While the next two verses (13-14) of the KJV try to

invest the text with the "daily sacrifices" in Israel again, the more important aspect of these verses is the 2300 days. This period has elicited all manner of speculation over the years. We have, therefore, elected to devote more space to it in the chapter to follow and will move now to the interpretive section of the chapter (verses 23-27) to consider information Gabriel adds concerning the "little horn." We emphasize again that the person Daniel describes in chapter 8 is the *same person he describes in Daniel 7 as the "little horn."*

Before proceeding, we should briefly restate what we know of Daniel's vision from Daniel 8:1-12. The Ram was the first actor to appear on the scene. As we noted, he represents the Medo-Persian Empire of the last days. Next came the Goat, who trampled the Ram and became "very great"; him we identified as a coalition of nations descended from Javan, whom the Ram provoked and who, in turn, destroyed the Ram. After "stamping" the Ram, the Goat's authority and power, symbolized by the great horn between his eyes, was broken, and four kingdoms stood out "from the nations" (verse 22). These four kingdoms ("four notable ones toward the four winds of heaven") existed until the "little horn" came on the scene. Gabriel takes up the subject of this "little horn" in Daniel 8:23-26, verses which provide an interpretation of what Daniel had originally observed in his vision. The "little horn" is now revealed to be a ruler, a "king of fierce countenance." Gabriel emphasizes that the events of the vision are to take place in the last days.

And In The Latter Time Of Their Kingdom

The Hebrew word translated "latter time" in Daniel

8:23 is "achariyth," meaning "the last or end, hence the future; also posterity: -(last, latter) end (time), hinder (utter) most."[20]   The frequent appearance of the phrases "latter time" and "the end" in the book of Daniel confirms that not only chapter 8 but the entire book contains truth primarily to be understood in the end time (Daniel 9:26; 11:6, 27, 35, 40, 45; 12:4, 6, 9, 13).   The word "achariyth" is used in many other biblical passages to indicate the absolute end:

Deuteronomy 11:12------end of the year.
Numbers 23:10------------end of a man's life.
Numbers 24:20------------end of a people's
                                         existence.
Deuteronomy 32:20,29--end condition of a
                                         nation, final lot.
Jeremiah 12:4; 31:17------end condition.

We must, therefore, assume that the final phase of these four kingdoms occurs, as Gabriel has emphasized in verse 17, "at the time of the end." The next phrase tell us, "when the transgressors are come to the full." There is certainly conclusiveness in that expression.

When The Transgressors Are Come To The Full.

The Hebrew word "pasha" from which we derive the word "transgressors," is a prime root meaning "to break away (from just authority). i.e. trespass, apostatize, quarrel; -offend, rebel, revolt, transgress (ion, or)."[21] The root denotes "to break allegiance," an act which results from sin and which applies to those who reject God's authority. To break allegiance is to exceed the limits of God's law, an action which dulls one's concept of right and wrong, while repeated transgression increases one's resistance to God's authority. In the last days, mankind will be guilty of all manner of transgression. Rebellion against God's standards will be the norm for those who follow the "little horn," just as it will be for their leader.

The phrase "to the full," used to describe the extent of this rebellion, comes from the Hebrew "tamam," which denotes completion. "Tamam" is a prime root meaning "to complete, in a good or bad sense, lit. or fig...accomplish...come to the full, have done, (come to an, have an, make an) end."[22] The implication of this phrase is that transgressors could not be any worse, any more wicked. As a bucket overflows when it is full, so sin will flood the world in the end times. This pervasive rebellion will signal impending judgment from God. Many examples of the judgment which follows such rebellion are recorded in the Bible, the following from Genesis 15 is one case in point:

Genesis 15:13   And he said unto Abram, know of a surety that thy seed shall be a stranger in a land that is not theirs, and shall serve them; and they shall afflict them four hundred years.

16   But in the fourth generation they shall come hither again: *for the iniquity of the Amorites is not yet full.*

Other times when God has allowed sin to run its course before He intervened are as follows:

1. The Genesis flood by which God destroyed the

world (Genesis 6:5-8).

2. The Tower of Babel, whence God scattered the people (Genesis 11:3-9).

3. The destruction of Sodom and Gomorrah (Genesis 19:24-25).

4. The destruction of the Egyptian army in the Red Sea (Exodus 14:26-28).

5. The destruction of the Northern Kingdom by Assyria in 722 B.C. (II Kings 17:5-7,18).

6. The destruction of Jerusalem and the Kingdom of Judah by Nebuchadnezzar in 586 B.C. (II Chronicles 36:15-21).

In each case, mankind was permitted a gracious period of time in which to alter his behaviour and, failing that, God's mercy and justice were vindicated as Lord of all His creation when the judgment fell. While some may complain of the inequity of judgment over love and mercy, we must recognize that in every act God undertakes, all of His attributes must be perfectly balanced at one and the same time. One attribute may not be emphasized to the exclusion of the others.

A King Of Fierce Countenance

We find that people are generally given the leader they deserve (Daniel 4:17). In the end time, because human iniquity will be so complete, the Lord will allow the worst person ever born to rule the world. While many cruel and despicable men have ruled over nations in the past, none has ever lived who is like the "little horn," the "king of fierce countenance" of Daniel 8:23, and the "vile person" of Daniel 11:21.

The Hebrew word "oz," translated "fierce" in this passage, comes from a prime root which means "to be stout (lit. or fig): harden, impudent, prevail, strengthen (self), be strong."[23] The word "countenance" here is translated from the plural of a Hebrew word meaning "face" and thus denotes many "faces". The "little horn" will present many "faces" (panim) to the world to convey the varieties of evil which define his character. HAW elaborates on the word "panim" as follows:

> This particular word always occurs in the plural, perhaps indicative of the fact that the face is a combination of a number of features. As we shall see below, the face identifies the person and reflects the attitude and sentiments of the person...It is only natural that the face was considered to be extraordinarily revealing vis-a-vis a man's emotions, moods, and dispositions. A "hard" face is indicative of defiance (Jer 5:3), impudence (Prov 7:13), ruthlessness (Deut 28:50). A "shining" face is evidence of joy (Job 29:24). A "shamed" face points to defeat, frustration, humiliation (II Samuel 19:5). A "flaming" face is one convulsed by terror (Isa 13:8). An "evil" face is marked by distress and anxiety (Gen 40:7).[24]

Experience tells us that a person's character and his moods can be read on his face. The "faces" of the "little horn" will all project a harsh, impudent, ruthless, and vile person determined to prevail, not only against men, but against God Himself.

And Understanding Dark Sentences.

The term "understanding" in verse 23 is translated from the Hebrew prime root, "biyn" that means to distinguish mentally between alternatives, to have insight and discernment. The phrase "dark sentences" is taken from the Hebrew word "chiydah" from a prime root "prop. to tie a knot, i.e. (fig) to propound a riddle: - put forth."[25] "Chiydah" is always used to describe the presentation of God's truth in such a manner that only those who know the Scriptures can discern its meaning. These two traits are unfortunately linked together in this passage about the "little horn": a harsh, impudent, ruthless countenance and an understanding of what God's Word teaches. While possessing Satan's knowledge of the Word, the "little horn" will also have Satan's one simple solution to any situation--his will. With no godly attributes of grace, love, mercy, justice, or righteousness to temper his decisions, the "little horn" will move to eliminate any and all who oppose him.

And His Power Shall Be Mighty But Not By His Own Power.

As we saw in verse 9, the "little horn" of Daniel's vision had power and strength which he exercised in many directions. Verse 24 too, emphasizes, "And his power was vast." We comprehend the source, not only of his power, but also of his willful disobedience to God's Word, from the next phrase: "but not by his own power." Empowered by Satan who, while knowing the Scriptures, will nevertheless desperately try to control all of God's earthly creation with the only means left at his command--cruelty and retaliation, the "little horn" is Satan's tool to vent his

133

wrath on Israel and the world. According to Revelation 12:2 Satan is well aware that his time is short:

> Revelation 12:12 ...Woe to the inhabitors of the earth and of the sea! for the devil is come down unto you, having great wrath, because he knoweth that he hath but a short time.

With Satan dictating his actions, the "little horn" will rule with a "rod of iron," not in righteousness as later the Lord Jesus Christ will in the Millennial kingdom, but in wickedness.

> Revelation 13:2 ...*And the dragon gave him his power, and his seat, and great authority.*

And He Shall Destroy Wonderfully

The word "destroy" in the next clause comes from the Hebrew word "shachath" a prime root meaning "to decay, i.e. cause) ruin (lit. or fig): batter, cast off, corrupt (er,thing), destroy (er, uction), lose, mar, perish, spill, spoiler, x utterly, waste (r)."[26] The verb form is used three times in the Bible to refer to moral danger or humiliation and is one of the principal words used to describe marring or corruption of earthly morality. Such connotations as "corrupt," "pervert," "snare," "waste," and "ruin," are prominent in this word.

The word translated "wonderfully" in the KJV, has caused some confusion among Bible scholars because in English it conveys the idea of something good or admirable, something that results in good fortune. Just the opposite will be true of the "little horn's" activities. When the word is applied to his powers of destruction that are defined here, it conveys the sense of "surpassing, extraordinary or exceptional evil," out of which nothing of merit can come. The "little horn's" corruption of mankind will be beyond comparison.

Prosper And Practice

We discussed both of these words in dealing with verse 12 (see our chapter 5). The "little horn" will prosper, or "push forward" successfully, in various ways. Jeremiah employs the word "prosper" to question God about the prosperity of the wicked. "Wherefore doth the way of the wicked prosper?" (Jeremiah 12:1). The same word is translated "ride prosperously" in Psalm 45:5 The use of the word gives us to understand that God will permit the "little horn" to succeed for a time in the course he has set for himself--to rule the world at the behest of Satan. Revelation 13:7 makes this delegated success quite clear:

> Revelation 13:7 And it was given unto him to make war with the saints, and to overcome them: and power was. given him over all kindreds, and tongues, and nations.

The period of the "little horn's" prosperity will also be the time of the "wrath of the lamb" when God is pouring forth his anger upon the whole earth. We read in the gospel of Matthew that:

Matthew 24:21 For then shall be great tribulation,
such as was not since the
beginning of the world to this time,
no, nor ever shall be.

Only Satan's instrument, blinded by his passionate
objectives could rejoice at "achievements" made during
such a time.

The next word translated "practice" in this passage
is from the same word seen in the previous chapter
meaning "to do" or "to make" in the broadest sense
and widest application. To accomplish, advance, be
occupied, or be busy are all acceptable translations.
With few obstacles in the path of his total control of
the world, the "little horn" will push forward rapidly
but only for a short time.

And Shall Destroy The Mighty And The Holy People

While we understand from Daniel 7:24 that the
"little horn" will come up in the northern kingdom as
the third ruler over the "diverse beast," and that he
will spend some time subduing "three kings" (the
rulers of Shem, Ham, and Japheth). Daniel 7:25; 12:7-
11 and Revelation 11:1-3; 13:5 tell us that the time
allotted to him in Scripture to persecute ("destroy") the
mighty and the holy people will be limited to three
and one-half years.

Daniel 7:25 And he shall speak great words
against the Most High, and shall wear
out the saints of the Most High, and
think to change the times and the laws;
and they shall be given into his hand

until *a time and times and the dividing of time.*

This brief period will probably begin with the events recorded in Daniel 11:29 as we will see shortly.

And Through His Policy

Daniel 8:25 introduces the means by which the "little horn" will accomplish his destructive ambitions: calculated deceit. Policy is translated from "sakal", a prime root meaning; "to be circumspect and hence intelligent."[27] HAW explains "sakal" as follows:

> "Sakal" relates to an intelligent knowledge of the reason. There is the process of thinking through a complex arrangement of thoughts resulting in a wise dealing and use of good practical common sense. Another end result is the emphasis upon being successful... Concerning an individual of the end time, it is said that he will through his shrewdness...cause deceit to succeed (Dan 8:25).[28]

A man of intelligence, able to think through complex situations, the "little horn" nevertheless will approach decisions with a shrewdness founded on deceit. How tragic that he will devote his intelligence entirely to criminal pursuits, but he is Satan's man.

He Shall Cause Craft To Prosper In His Hand

The word "craft" in this passage is translated from the Hebrew "mirmah" a word which conveys the sense of "deception, fraud;-craft, deceit (-ful,-fully), false, feigned, guile, subtilly, treachery."[29] Just as Satan "beguiled" Eve in the garden to sin (Genesis 3:13), so the "little horn" will beguile his followers, but treachery is in his heart. The Apostle Paul warned the Thessalonians to beware of the tactics that may be expected from the "man of sin":

II Thessalonians 2:9   Even him, whose coming is after the working of Satan with all power and signs and lying wonders,

10   And with all deceivableness of unrighteousness in them that perish; because they received not the love of the truth, that they might be saved.

11   And for this cause God shall send them strong delusion, that they should believe a lie.

The deceitfulness of the "little horn," will be planned, promoted, and controlled by Satan and his demonic realm as predicted in Revelation 13:2b:

Revelation 13:2b   ...And the dragon gave him his power, and his seat, and great authority.

He Shall Magnify Himself In His Heart

The word "magnify" in this passage is translated from the Hebrew word, "gadol," which appears in verse 11. As we noted earlier, the word is causative and in the imperfect, a grammatical construction which loosely approximates the English future tense.[30] In his lust for glory, the "little horn" will exalt himself ("cause to be great") beyond any man who has ever existed. Just as Satan sought to rise above God (Isaiah 14:12-14), so will the "insignificant horn" seek the same status:

> II Thessalonians 2:4 Who opposeth and exalteth himself above all that is called God, or that is worshipped; so that he as God sitteth in the temple of God, shewing himself that he is God.

By Peace Shall Destroy Many

The Hebrew word translated " peace" in this passage is "shalom". Declaring himself the "Prince of Peace" promised in the biblical record, the "little horn" will deceive his followers into thinking him capable of bringing peace, that most elusive commodity, to the world. With mankind so desperate for peace, the "little horn" will lure many to their destruction.

He Shall Also Stand Up Against The Prince Of Princes

The original Hebrew word order for this clause is, "Against the prince of princes he shall stand," with the phrase "prince of princes" appearing, as it should, in the emphatic position at the beginning of the sentence. Prince of princes, King of kings and Lord of lords--all these are titles given to the beloved Son of

God. Thus it is against the Lord Jesus Christ that the "little horn" will take his final stand.

But He Shall Be Broken Without Hands

The word "broken" is translated from the Hebrew "shabar" meaning "to break in pieces, crush, destroy, ruin."[31] In this passage the verb describes God's judgmental, punitive action. "Shabar" is found twenty-eight times in the prophets where the word is applied to the impending destruction of both the northern and southern kingdoms. Keil explains "broken without hands" as follows:

> He shall be destroyed without hands," i.e., he shall be destroyed, not by the hand of man, but by God.[32]

None other than the Son of God will come with the armies of heaven to destroy the kingdom of the "little horn." Revelation 19 vividly pictures this climatic moment:

Revelation 19:11 And I saw heaven opened, and behold a white horse; and he that sat upon him was called Faithful and True, and in righteousness he doth judge and make war.

15 And out of his mouth goeth a sharp sword, that with it he should smite the nations, and he shall rule them with a rod of iron; and he treadeth the winepress of the fierceness and

140

wrath of Almighty God.

16 And he hath on his vesture and
on his thigh a name written,
KING OF KINGS, AND LORD
OF LORDS.

19 And I saw the beast, and the
kings of the earth, and their
armies, gathered together to
make war against him that sat on
the horse, and against his army.

20 And the beast was taken, and
with him the false prophet that
wrought miracles before him,
with which he deceived them
that received the mark of the
beast, and them that worshipped
his image. These both were cast
alive into a lake of fire burning
with brimstone.

With the defeat of the "little horn," Satan will be
banished to the bottomless pit, his power restrained
for the period of the Millennium as recorded in
Revelation 20:

Revelation 20:1 And I saw an angel come down
from heaven, having the key of
the bottomless pit and a great
chain in his hand.

2 And he laid hold on the dragon,
that old serpent, which is the
Devil, and Satan, and bound him

> a thousand years,

> 3 And cast him into the bottomless pit, and shut him up, and set a seal upon him, that he should deceive the nations no more, till the thousand years should be fulfilled: and after that he must be loosed a little season.

With Satan banished, the Lord Jesus will reign in righteousness for a thousand years. Pentecost explains the necessity for this righteous period during which all sources of temptation have been removed:

> So that there can be a full manifestation of righteousness and a test of humanity apart from external temptation, Satan must be removed from the sphere.[33]

This time of righteousness (the Millennial Kingdom) would not be possible apart from the sharp sword of the Word of God.

And The Vision Of The Evening And The Morning Which Was Told Is True

Gabriel's confirmation to Daniel that the content of both visions (chapters 7 and 8) are truth should strengthen the faith of God's people. The word "true" in this passage comes from the Hebrew word "'emeth," which means "stability; fig. certainty, truth, trustworthiness:-assured (-ly), established, faithful, right, sure, true (-ly,-th), verity."[34] The never-failing trustworthiness of the Word of God is an unwavering source of strength and comfort to those who place their faith in it.

Wherefore Shut Thou Up The Vision

Gabriel's injunction to Daniel to "shut up" the vision is preceded by the Hebrew word "attah," which is the Hebrew second person singular translated "you," instead of the word "wherefore" which is not even in the Hebrew text.   "Attah" is the emphatic "you" translated here "thou." But because of the emphasis, the sentence should be read, "And *you* shut up the vision." The expression "shut up" comes from the Hebrew word "satham" a prime root which means "to stop up; by impl. to repair; fig. to keep secret:-closed up, hidden, secret, shut out (up), stop."[35]   The meaning of the word clearly implies that the interpretation of Daniel has been reserved for the distant future. The language is even more explicit in Daniel 12:

Daniel 12:4 But thou, O Daniel, shut up the
words, seal the book, even to the
time of the end: many shall run to
and fro, and knowledge shall be
increased.

Although the book has been available to scholars for 25 centuries, a full grasp of the interpretation is only possible in the last days. The book was initially written for the instruction of and warning to Israel who were in captivity at the time of Daniel's writing. In spite of God's warning, the people quickly broke fellowship with God after He returned them to the land. Israel transgressed His Word to such an extent that God rejected first their worship (Malachi 1-2) and finally the nation (Matthew 23:37-39).

Matthew 23:38 Behold, your house is left unto you desolate.

During this interim period between Malachi and Matthew (the intertestamental period), Judaism, a false religion of the Pharisees, assumed the spiritual responsibility for the nation, and this "leaven of the Pharisees" was primarily responsible for Israel's rejection and execution of the promised Messiah, the Lord Jesus Christ.

After this Church Age closes with the Rapture of the Church, the Lord will again offer His Kingdom to Israel, this time through the 144,000 sealed Jews (Revelation 7:4) and the two witnesses (Revelation 11:3-12). A correct interpretation of the book of Daniel will be crucial then for the instruction of faithful Jews as well as for Gentiles saved during that period. Israel's rebirth in 1948 signaled God's intention to fulfill His unconditional promises to the nation. Believing that the time of the end is approaching, we suggest that God has now removed the seal on the book making a true understanding of Daniel's prophecies possible at last. With the seal removed, students of the Word can explore the truth which has been "shut" and "sealed" since shortly after Israel's return from Babylonian exile.

For It Shall Be For Many Days

"Shall be" is in italics to indicate it has been added by the translators. The literal reading is, "For it is for many days," a general statement indicating many days yet future. Daniel, along with other leaders of Israel, was longing for a fulfillment of the promised kingdom when the seventy years of captivity were finished, but

Gabriel was warning Daniel that the time of the end was not yet near. Because the seventy weeks of years for Israel revealed in Daniel's vision of chapter 9 had not yet been given, the phrase "many days" is a generalized term for an indefinite period of time yet future. Thereafter, statements such as, "at the time of the end, the vision," (verse 17) or, "at the time appointed, the end" (verse 19) are much more specific as to the time when the vision will be fulfilled.

And I Daniel Fainted...And I Was Astonished At The Vision

As we noted in an earlier chapter, when Daniel understood the import of his vision, Daniel was sick for a time, a sickness which he described as "fainting." After recovering from his illness, Daniel went about the king's business, still stunned and devastated by the content of his vision. The word "astonished" in the passage is translated from the Hebrew word "shamen," a prime root which means "to stun (intrans. grow numb),i.e. devastate or (fig) stupefy (both usually in a passive sense): make amazed, be astonied, (be an) astonish (-ment), (be, bring into, unto, lay, lie, make) desolate (-ion, places), be destitute, destroy (self), (lay, make lie,) waste, wonder."[36] As an elder in Israel, Daniel was emotionally involved with his nation's fate. The understanding he had gained of the two visions and especially the detail revealed in the second vision, left Daniel with knowledge which devastated him.

But None Understood (It)

No one in all of Israel could grasp what Daniel experienced as he viewed the future of his nation and the world. The identity of the "diverse beast," the struggle of the Ram and the Goat, and the persecution under the "little horn"--all these weighed heavily upon his consciousness. Yet none but Daniel understood: he bore the burden of God's revelation alone.

Summary

We identified present-day Iran as the Ram, destroyed in the last days by the Goats--Gentiles descended from Javan. The four kingdoms symbolized by the four beasts in Daniel 7 and the four "notable ones" in Daniel 8 represent the descendants of the three sons of Noah--Shem, Ham, and Japheth--polarized in the end time, along with the northern kingdom of Israel (symbolized by the 10 horns on the "diverse" beast in Daniel 7:7). The power of these first three kingdoms (those of Shem, Ham, and Japheth) will be "plucked up" by the fourth (that of the "little horn") and all will be consolidated into the kingdom of the Antichrist, or "the beast out of the sea" (Revelation 13:1). Empowered by Satan (Revelation 13:2) the "little horn," the "Antichrist," will rule the world with an iron fist for 42 months (3 1/2 years); but at the very end he will be "broken without hand" by the personal intervention of the Son of God and cast into the lake of fire (Revelation 19:20) along with the false prophet. The Lord Jesus Christ will then be established as King over all the earth.

End Notes

1. Keil & Delitszch, page 295
2. Unger, page 456
3. Josephus, page IX
4. Ibid, page 192

5. Strong, page 12
6. BDB, page 40
7. Strong, page 98
8. Ibid, page 85
9. Walvoord, Daniel, page 186
10. HAW, page 750
11. Strong, page 63
12. HAW, page 837
13. Ibid, page 838
14. Strong, page 125
15. HAW, page 789
16. Strong, page 53
17. Ibid, page 99
18. HAW, 766
19. Strong, 92
20. Ibid, page 11
21. Ibid, page 97
22. Ibid, page 125
23. Ibid, page 87
24. HAW, 727
25. Strong, page 20
26. Ibid, page 36
27. Ibid, page 115
28. Ibid, page 116
29. HAW, page 876
30. Strong, page 73
31. Weingreen, page 75
32. Keil & Delitzsch, page 318
33. Pentecost, page 477
34. Strong, page 14
35. Ibid, page 84
36. Ibid, page 118

Chapter 6

How Long The Vision?

Daniel 8:13   Then I heard one saint speaking, and another saint said unto that certain *saint* which spake, How long *shall be* the vision *concerning* the daily *sacrifice*, and the transgression of desolation, to give both the sanctuary and the host to be trodden under foot?

    14   And he said unto me, Unto two thousand and three hundred days; then shall the sanctuary be cleansed.

As we open this section on the 2300 days, we must note first that Daniel does not refer to himself by name ("he said to me")but refers to a certain one or particular one making the inquiry. This usage is similar to that of John the Apostle who, rather than name himself as the one standing by the cross, referred simply to "the disciple" (John 19:26-27).

Next, it is apparent that the wording of this passage has caused much confusion among Bible scholars. In the KJV of verse 13 five words appear in italics, to indicate that they were added to the text by translators for clarification. While such additions are meant to clarify the text, in the above case they actually confuse the matter. Daniel's vision had nothing to do with the daily sacrifices in Israel. Instead, Daniel asks the angel how long it will take (the duration)for certain events he had seen in his vision to come to an end.[1] He asks for answers to a three-part question:

1. How long will the events of the vision endure?

2. How long will the rebellion and apostasy of the "little horn" endure?

3. How long will the faithful suffer?

We will discuss each of these questions in sequence.

(1) In the first phrase, "How long?", the words translated "how long" (or better yet "until when"), comes from the Hebrew "ad," "prop. a (peremptory) terminus, i.e. (by imp.) duration, in the sense of advance or perpetuity,"[1] and from the Hebrew "mathay" (an unused root, meaning to extend) "prop. extent (of time)...when (either rel. or interrog.): - long, when."[2] As we explained earlier when we discussed the same word which appears in verses 11 and 12, the word rendered "daily" in our English translations is derived from the Hebrew word "tamiyd," which means continuance, duration, stretched out. Since no mention of "sacrifice" appears in the text, we prefer to translate the word "tamiyd" according to its normal usage. Instead of "how long shall be the vision concerning the daily sacrifice," then, we should read, "how long the duration of the vision?" or literally, "until when is the vision stretched out?" Daniel was satisfied that he knew what was going to happen to the world in the last days. These events had been

---

[1] Some commentators believe that in this passage Daniel is reporting a conversation he overheard between two angels.

shown him in the vision. His attention here is drawn neither to the traumatic events surrounding the battle between the Ram and the Goat nor to the rise of the "four notable ones" (he already had grasped the significance of the "four notable ones" in the vision in chapter 7), but rather to the climatic end-time events involving his own people--the desolating transgressions, the trampling of the holy place and the host of the faithful remnant. His concern is the duration of that time period. How long will it last?

(2) The KJV translation of the second part of verse 13, Daniel's inquiry concerning the "transgression of desolation," is a good one. The word transgression comes from the Hebrew word "pasha" a prime root which means (through the idea of expansion); "to break away (from just authority), i.e. trespass, apostatize, quarrel; - offend, rebel, revolt, transgress (ion,or)."[3] Daniel's vision foretold the establishment of a rebellious society which would "break away" from God's authority and initiate a lawless regime bent on destruction. Here Daniel seeks specific information about that society: the duration of the rebellion and apostasy which will devastate the sacred place of God (Jerusalem) and trample God's people. Verse 23 records the answer to this part of Daniel's question: that the time will begin when "transgressors are come to the full," or complete and ready for judgment (Daniel 8:23).

The word "of" in this passage comes from a Hebrew verb "nathan," a prime root: meaning "to give, used with great latitude of application (put, make, etc)."[4] Elsewhere in the KJV the word "nathan" is rendered "deliver, bestow, suffer (allow), commit." Thus an accurate rendering of this passage is "transgression making (or giving) desolation."

The word translated "desolation" here is the Hebrew verb "shamem," a prime root meaning "to stun (or intrans. grow numb), i.e. devastate or (fig) stupefy (both usually in a passive sense): make amazed, be astonied, (be an) astonish (ment), (be, bring into, unto, lay, lie, make) desolate (ion, places), be destitute, destroy (self), (lay, lie, make) waste, wonder."[5] The "little horn's" acts of corruption and brutality, both in Israel and in the rest of the world, will stun mankind with their devastation.

(3) The third part of Daniel's query, which the KJV renders, "Sanctuary and the host trodden under foot?", concerns Jerusalem and the faithful band of Israelites to be trampled by the armies of the "little horn." Daniel wants to know the duration of their suffering. Gabriel corroborates this attack on God's people in verse 24 and again in Daniel 11:33 and 12:7 and other biblical passages refer to this final persecution. This is the "time of Jacob's trouble" predicted in Jeremiah 30:7.

> Zechariah 14:2 For I will gather all nations against Jerusalem to battle; and the city shall be taken, and the houses rifled, and the women ravished; and half of the city shall go forth into captivity, and the residue of the people shall not be cut off from the city.

> Revelation 12:17 And the dragon was wroth with the woman, and went to make war with the remnant of her

seed, which keep the
commandments of God, and
have the testimony of Jesus
Christ.

Revelation 13:7 And it was given unto him to
make war with the saints, and to
overcome them...

The Answer to Daniel's Question!

A literal rendering of the Hebrew text in 8:14--the
answer to Daniel's question in verse 13--reads: "Unto
two thousand and three hundred evenings and
mornings; and the holy place shall be righteous."
When divided by 360 (the number of days in a Jewish
year) the 2300 days given in answer come to *six years,
four months, and twenty days.* As can be expected,
scholars speculating on the import of this number
have come up with a variety of explanations; the
principal of these and our alternative we will outline
below.

Advent Theory

The Seventh Day Adventist denomination was
established on the basis of one explanation of the
number given in answer to Daniel's query. With the
seventy weeks of years mentioned in Daniel 9 in
mind, a group of scholars led by William Miller (1782-
1849) concluded that the "evenings and mornings" of
Daniel 8 were also to be measured in years. Believing
that each day represented a year and beginning with
a date in the reign of Cyrus, Miller predicted that the
twenty three hundred years would end in 1843 with
the Rapture of the Church. Deciding that his

calculations were off by one year when the expected Rapture did not occur, Miller rescheduled the event for 1844, but was again disappointed. Miller's followers eventually formed the Adventist denomination which remains a segment of the religious scene even today.

Several problems render the Advent theory inadmissible, the most obvious of which is that the Rapture did not take place when Miller predicted it would. In addition, Daniel, a Jewish prophet, never had the Church in view, and thus its Rapture was not an object of the prophecy given to him. While Miller equated the 2300 days with 2300 years, the Hebrew text reads "2300 evenings and mornings" just as it does in Genesis 1-2, where the creation account is related. We may safely assume that the days Gabriel mentioned in Daniel 8:14 are also to be understood as 24-hour days. There is nothing in the Hebrew text which would warrant stretching for an unusual interpretation. To the question of Daniel 9:24 which most conservatives interpret as speaking of seventy weeks of years rather than weeks of days, we direct the reader's attention to the Hebrew vocabulary used in Daniel 9. There the words "shabuiym shibiym nuchthk" meaning "seventy sevens are determined" appears--not the words "ereb boqer" meaning "evening and morning" as in Daniel 8. We must conclude that Gabriel was speaking of 2300 twenty-four-hour days.

Half-Day Theory

Because Daniel used the terms "evening and morning," some scholars divide the 2300 days in half to equal 1150 days, theorizing that this passage alludes to a shortened "great Tribulation," that is, the last half

153

of the seventieth week of Daniel. This theory is based on the two daily sacrifices, offered morning and evening in Israel according to the Law.

This explanation also misses the mark for several reasons. First, as we noted earlier, while the KJV inserts the word "sacrifice" into the text of verse 13 to clarify the meaning, no word which can be so translated is present in the original language. The passage simply refers to a 24-hour day and not to the evening and morning sacrifices. Moreover, the number 1150 falls 110 days short of the 42 months (three and one-half years or 1260 days) allotted to the Antichrist in *many* scriptural passages.[2] Daniel 9 tells us the seventy weeks are "determined," which means that they will not be altered. They cannot therefore be the "shortened" days of Matthew 24:22 as this half-day theory would imply.

Antiochus Epiphanes Theory

Because of their involvement with the intertestamental history of Antiochus Epiphanes, the traditional conservative community postulate the following theory: The span of time from the murder of Onias III, the priest in the line of Aaron, in 171 B.C. and the installation of an impostor (Menelaus) to the death of Antiochus Epiphanes in 164 B.C. is adequate time for fulfillment of the 2300 days mentioned in Daniel 8:14. The death of Antiochus would signal the

---

[2] The 1260 days are determined, meaning fixed, and will not be changed. This period is identified in several places in the Bible: Daniel 7:25; 9:24; 12:7,11; Revelation 12:14; 13:5.

cleansing of the Temple and the people's return to worship.

We have already refuted much of the error in this theory in our writings, where we point out repeatedly that the Bible is its own best interpreter, and does not mention Antiochus Epiphanes but does specifically state that the vision is for the "time of the end" (Daniel 8:17b). In our books, we identified the source for this view as Porphyry, a pagan philosopher, whose theory was later adopted by Jerome and we observed that God does not reveal the meaning of prophecy to pagans. Another problem with this theory involves dating. Antiochus probably died in 163 B.C. according to the Cambridge Ancient History who further states that there is no way to arrive at accurate dates for this period because secular history of the time is so sketchy and untrustworthy. Further, the desecration of the Temple did not occur until December 25, 167 B.C., when the sacrifices in the temple ceased and the Greek altar was erected. The actual desecration lasted approximately three years, not 2300 days. And finally, Scripture points this passage to the time of the end, when the Lord Jesus Christ will face this "king of fierce countenance" (Daniel 8:23) at the battle of Armageddon: "He shall stand up against the Prince of Princes; but he shall be broken without hand" (Daniel 8:25b) Antiochus Epiphanes never fulfilled this prophecy.[3]

---

[3] In order to avoid this problem traditionalists divide Daniel 8 into two parts and claim a dual fulfillment. According to this theory, the first part of the chapter alludes to Antiochus Epiphanes as "the desolator" because of his desecration of the Temple, while the second part

Short Time Theory

One group of interpreters believe that the 2300 days mentioned in Daniel 8:14 represent the seventieth week of Daniel 9 shortened by God to give the people of the world relief from a devastation that would otherwise destroy all flesh. The proof text for this theory is Matthew 24:21-22:

> Matthew 24:21 For then shall be great tribulation, such as was not since the beginning of the world to this time, no, nor ever shall be.

> 22 And except those days should be shortened, there should no flesh be saved: but for the elect's sake those days shall be shortened.

The above might indeed provide a good scriptural explanation of Daniel's 2300 days if, in truth, seven full years of the seventieth week remained to be fulfilled. But as we demonstrated in our previous book, *The Seventy Weeks of Daniel*, the language of the text in Daniel 9:27 indicates that half of that final week was fulfilled in the three and one-half years of our Lord's ministry. Only the 42 months (3 and 1/2

---

looks forward to the greater desolator to come, the one who is called Antichrist, the man of sin, the beast, or the "little horn" of Daniel 7. We contend that the "little horn" of Daniel 7 and the "little horn" of Daniel 8 are one and the same. Antiochus Epiphanes has no place in the prophecy of Daniel.

156

years) allotted to the Antichrist's rule remain of that week. And further, as we did in our discussion of the half-day theory, we must emphasize that Daniel 9 declares the entire seventy weeks to be "determined." Since those days cannot be "shortened," we must look for another explanation of the 2300 days. When in God's time it becomes proper, even necessary for His own to understand His plan, God does not attempt to hide from them the outline of end-time events. Those who belong to Him have been told that they need not grope in darkness but can know the truth as "children of the day."

> I Thessalonians 5:4 But ye, brethren, are not in darkness, that that day should overtake you as a thief.
>
> 5 Ye are the children of light, and the children of the day: we are not of the night, nor of darkness.
>
> 6 Therefore let us not sleep, as do others; but let us watch and be sober.

As we approach the end of the Church Age, believers may enjoy inside knowledge of climatic world events to come.

A Scriptural Alternative

The question Daniel asks in verse 13 is "until when." The answer he receives in verse 14 is 2300 evenings and mornings. Calculated by the Jewish calendar of 360 days per year, 2300 24-hour days equal six years, four months, and twenty days. Does this time frame include those events of the vision which involve the battle between the Ram (Iran), and the Goat, (the descendants of Javan in the western world)? Does it include the formation of the four "notable" kingdoms which we have previously identified as the descendants of Shem, Ham, Japheth and the beast "diverse from them all" that stand up out of the vacuum created after the battle between the Ram and the Goats (Daniel 7)? *Probably not!* The wording of the text tells us that the specific duration of time Daniel inquired about was that of the devastating transgression of God's holy place and the trampling underfoot of His people. This interpretation is entirely consistent with Daniel's concerns in other portions of the book. In chapter 7 verse 19 Daniel was eager to "know the truth of the fourth beast" because he understood that it would stamp the "residue" (the faithful remnant of Israel) underfoot. Daniel's prayer for his people and for the Holy City (recorded in Daniel 9) and his deep mourning for his people (Daniel 10:2) display his commitment to pray for both his nation and Jerusalem. Daniel's overriding concern was to learn the specific details of God's consummation of His covenant with Israel. We must be equally specific in our interpretation of Daniel's vision.

Since 2300 days is more than that allotted in Scripture (1260 days, or 42 months, or 3 1/2 years) to Satan's control of the Beast (Antichrist; see Revelation 13:1-2), we must look for an explanation of the number which fits all the demands of Scripture. That explanation is available to us through the additional revelation recorded in Daniel 11. The first "king of the north" of Daniel 11 is the first ruler over the "diverse beast" of Daniel 7. (A full explanation of the "diverse beast" can be found in our previous book in this series, *The Four Beasts Of Daniel 7.*) This king will come on the scene to fill the vacuum created by the Goat's destruction of the Ram as the four "notable ones" form "toward the four winds of heaven" (Daniel 11:4). According to Daniel 11:13, this king will rule for a few years before the second ruler comes on the scene briefly (see Daniel 11:20). Daniel 11:21 then introduces a "vile person" the same person as the "little horn" of Daniel 7 and 8, better known as the Antichrist or Beast of Revelation 13. This third ruler will gain the support of the ten northern tribes by flattery and by promising peace (see Daniel 11:21), but in reality, he will consolidate his power by force (Daniel 11:22-24;), subduing the first three beasts (Shem, Ham, and Japheth), thereby gaining world-wide recognition and power (Daniel 7:8,20,24; Revelation 13:4). His power plays against the other nations of the world occur even as this "vile person" consolidates his position as ruler in the northern kingdom (Daniel 11:22-24). We have previously mentioned this take over in our interpretation of Daniel 8:9. His position established, however, the "little horn" will then turn his attention toward the southern kingdom and the "king of the south" (see Daniel 11:25).

At this point in his assault he will be simply another aggressor against God's people and the Holy place just as his predecessor, the first "king of the north" had been (see Daniel 11:11-14), but not yet indwelt by Satan. With his invasion of the south, however, the 2300 days of God's timetable for the devastating transgression and trampling of that which is sacred begins. Daniel 11:25-28 suggest several great battles, the "little horn" or "king of the north" emerging with great riches and increasing antagonism toward the holy covenant (verse 28), but with his final end prepared "at the time appointed" (verse 27). Daniel 8:9-10 records the change in tempo of the "little horn's" progress. While Daniel 8:9 shows him arising and growing "great", verse 10 begins the correlation with the "war in heaven" passage of Revelation 12:6-14. Cast out of heaven, Satan will enter into the "little horn" signalling the start of the Antichrist's allotted 42 months of power. Now possessed by Satan and committed to Satan's intent to destroy the mighty and holy people, the Antichrist will concentrate his attack on the Southern Kingdom and Jerusalem.

While the progress of the 2300 days begins in Daniel 11:25, the specific time allotted to the Antichrist after he is indwelt by Satan (42 months) begins in Daniel 11:29. Verse 29 declares this to be *"the time appointed"* and tells us that this time will be completely different from the "former" or the "latter," (referring to the campaigns of the first king of the "diverse beast" and the first campaign of the "little horn" toward the south, respectively; see verses 13-15 and 25). Daniel 11:29 through Daniel 12:2, however, speaks of the specific period of the "time of Jacob's trouble," brought about by Satan's personal control of the "insignificant horn." Much of the confusion arises out of conflicting terms which identify the end-time period and the reign of the Antichrist. Such terms as "the seventieth week of Daniel 9," the 2300 days of Daniel 8:14, the "wrath of the Lamb" in Revelation 6:16-16, the "great tribulation" in Matthew 24:21, the "time of Jacob's trouble" in Jeremiah 30:7 all need definition. Assuming for years that the "great tribulation" period predicted by the Lord in Matthew

24:21 is equivalent to the last 3 and 1/2 years of a seventieth week of seven full years, we have ignored our Lord's clear and unambiguous promise that "those days shall be shortened." But since the 42 months (1260 days) of Satan's control of the Antichrist are said in Daniel 9 to be "determined" and thus cannot be altered, the Lord surely was not referring to that period in Matthew 24:21. The time of great tribulation and affliction which Jesus referred to *is* the 2300 days. It is equally the period of the "wrath of the Lamb" (Revelation 6), which begins prior to the manifestation of the Antichrist under Satan's control in Revelation 13 and continues through his allotted 42 months. The days of the "wrath of the Lamb," prior to Satan's control of the Antichrist will, by God's grace, be shortened. There will be no quarter given by Satan once he takes possession of the "little horn." He will demand his right to the full 3 1/2 years already "determined."

Only the last 42 months of the Antichrist's reign can justifiably be called "the time of Jacob's trouble," for only with the war in heaven will Satan enter into the "little horn" transforming him into the Beast of Revelation 13, committed to Satan's agenda to destroy God's chosen people. Note the chronology of Revelation: chapter 4 presents the Church in heaven, chapter 5 presents the Lamb as the One worthy to open the scroll and break the seals, and chapters 6-11 present the seals and trumpets of tribulation and affliction beginning to break over the world. Not until Revelation 13, *after* the war in heaven passage of Revelation 12, is the Beast introduced with his allotted 42 months of power. The chronology and time given in Scripture for these events must be considered in an accurate interpretation.

In summary, the 2300 days of Daniel 8 begins in Daniel 8:9 with the 42 months of Satan's control beginning in verse 10. In Daniel 11, the 2300 days begins in verse 25, with the 42 months of Satan's control beginning in verse 29 and continuing to the end of Daniel 12:2. The 2300 days refer to both "the wrath of the Lamb" (Revelation 6) and "the great tribulation" (Matthew 24). Only the last 42 months or 1260 days of this 2300-day period are allotted to the "little horn" in his role as the Beast of Revelation 13 empowered by Satan. This final 42 months represents the last half of the seventieth week of Daniel 9 and the "time of Jacob's trouble." Properly differentiating these terms will help us understand end-time events. As we have mentioned before, from Daniel 7:1 to 12:13 we see a progressive unfolding of information concerning these significant mileposts of the end-time.

As late as Daniel 12:6-7, we find the prophet inquiring how much time will be required to fulfill these wonders. There he is told that a time, times, and an half will be required to break up the power of the holy people--the 3 and 1/2 years of the "time of Jacob's trouble," the allotted period for the Antichrist, and the last half of the seventieth week of Daniel 9. Of mathematical necessity Daniel's 2300 days must start 1040 days prior to the 3 and 1/2 years and is the only period which can be "shortened," since we are told in Daniel 9 that the entire seventy weeks have already been "determined" by God. The word "determined" means a decision which has been "cut and incised to the point that it is unalterable". Those final 3 and 1/2 years cannot and will not be shortened.

The Holy Place Made Righteous (Justified)

Derived from only two Hebrew words, "tsadaq" and "qadesh," the clause, "then shall the sanctuary be cleansed" would literally read, "and the Holy Place righteous." The verb "tsadaq", is a prime root which means "to be (causative, make) right (in a moral or forensic sense): cleanse, clear self, (be, do) just (ice, ify, ify self), (be, turn to) righteous (ness)."[6] This reflexive verb emphasizes the second word of the clause, "qadesh", meaning "a sacred place or thing; rarely abstract; sanctity:-consecrated (thing), dedicated (thing), hallowed (thing), holiness, (x most) holy (x day, portion, thing), saint, sanctuary."[7] We take this word to refer to the sacred place dedicated and consecrated to the worship of God, that is, Mount Zion, the dwelling place of the King. Jerusalem will be made righteous by the personal presence of Jesus Christ who will institute an earthly kingdom and will govern the whole world according to the norms and standards of God.

In Daniel 9:24, one of the barriers to restoring the nation of Israel to its proper spiritual position will be overcome by the "anointing of the Most Holy." As we pointed out in our book, *The Seventy Weeks of Daniel*, this anointing will take place at the installation of the Lord Jesus Christ as King. The use of "qadesh" then in 8:14 places an emphasis on this same time when the blaspheming of God's name and the things of God will come to an end and righteousness will prevail: at the anointing of the Lord Jesus Christ as King in the place long sacred to God--Mt Zion.

Interpretation By Gabriel

Daniel 8:15-19 tell us that Daniel actively sought the interpretation of his vision and was rewarded when God sent Gabriel to give him the answer. Each time Daniel asked for the interpretation of a vision, he received immediate divine assistance:

Daniel 2:19 Then was the secret revealed unto Daniel in a night vision...

Daniel 7:16 I came near unto one of them that stood by, and asked him the truth of all this. So he told me, and made me know the interpretation of the things.

Daniel 8:15 And it came to pass, when I, even I Daniel, had seen the vision, and sought for the meaning, then, behold, there stood before me as the appearance of a man.

16 ...and said, Gabriel, make this man to understand the vision.

Daniel 9:21 Yea, whiles I was speaking in prayer, even the man Gabriel, whom I had seen in the vision at the beginning...

22 And he informed me, and talked with me, and said, O Daniel, I am now come forth to give thee skill and understanding.

Daniel 10:11 And he said unto me, O Daniel, a man greatly beloved, understand the words that I speak unto thee...

14 Now I am come to make thee
   understand what shall befall thy
   people in the latter days...

In Daniel 8:16, as in Daniel 9:21, Gabriel is specifically
identified as God's messenger to Daniel and in each
passage Gabriel uses the Hebrew word "biyn,"
translated "understand," a prime root which means "to
separate mentally (or distinguish)."[8] In both chapters,
Daniel is to distinguish not only the significant content
of the vision but also the period of time of the vision's
fulfillment.

The Time Of The End

Before giving the prophet an interpretation,
Gabriel made sure that Daniel understood that his
vision was for the end time. Three times in Daniel 8
Gabriel emphasized the time element that is
indispensable to a correct interpretation of the vision
(emphasis ours):

Daniel 8:17 Understand, O Son of man: for *at
          the time of the end (shall be)
          the vision.*

       19 And he said, Behold, I will make
          thee know what shall be in *the last
          end of the indignation: for at the time
          appointed the end (shall be).*

       26 *for it (shall be) for many days.*

In each verse, the words "shall be" are printed in
parenthesis to indicate that they do not appear in the
original language, but the content leaves no doubt that

Daniel's vision is for the end time.

The Last End of the Indignation

In Daniel 8:19 the word "last" is translated from
the Hebrew word "achar", which means "after-part,
end, of time, latter part or actual close; of year (Dt
11:12); of a man's life (Nu 23:10, Pr 5:11); Isa 41:22, in
the end of the days, a prophetic phrase denoting the
final period of history as far as the speaker's
perspective reaches... Jer 50:12, the last, hindermost."[9]

"Indignation" is translated from the Hebrew word
"za'am" a prime root, "prop. to foam at the mouth, i.e.,
to be enraged:-abhor, abominable, (be) angry, defy,
(have) indignation."[10] The root idea expressed by
"za'am" is intense anger, by implication God's anger
to the fullest; by combining this word with the word
"last" mentioned above, Gabriel clearly means to speak
of the last time God will judge Israel and the nations;
the use of this same word to respond to Babylon the
great, the mother of harlots, at the end of the
Tribulation suggests that both actions will occur in the
same time frame (emphasis ours):

> Revelation 16:19 And the great city was divided
> into three parts, and the cities
> of the nations fell: and great
> Babylon came in remembrance
> before God, to give unto her the
> cup of the wine of the *fierceness
> of his wrath.*

At no other time in history will God display such
anger, such indignation, against mankind's sin.
Revelation 16:19 echoes the climatic event prophesied

in Daniel 8:19.

At The Time Appointed The End

The KJV derives its translation of the phrase "for at the time appointed the end *shall be*" from just two Hebrew words, "mo'ed" and "qets." (Because it appears in italics, we know that the verb "shall be" has been added to the text for clarification.) "Mo'ed" is translated "appointed sign, appointed season, place of assembly, set feast."[11] Used reflexively, the action is thrown back upon the subject, and expresses, with some pathos, the interest, or satisfaction, or completeness with which the action is accomplished. Here the word expresses, with God's reluctant satisfaction, the finality of His indignation against both Israel and the nations for their unceasing rebellion.

The word translated "end" in this passage comes from "qets" a prime root meaning "to chop off (lit. or fig.): cut (asunder, in pieces, off), utmost,"[12] or "to sever," i.e. to separate in two."[13] The time when God manifests His anger against both apostate Israel and the nations will be the cut off period--the absolute end of the "transgression which maketh desolation." The remnant of Israel, those who have been faithful, will move from this period of extreme persecution into the Millennium. The difference between the two periods is as different as that between night and day. Transgression, desolation, and suffering will be followed by the rule of the Righteous King when faithful Israel, along with the saved of the nations, will experience God's complete blessing.

The Rapture Of The Church

As we mentioned earlier, Daniel was a Jewish prophet, concerned neither with the Church nor with events of the Church Age; he wrote only of those things that involve the nation of Israel. It is natural, however, for believers in the Church Age to wonder where the Church fits into the end-time events of Daniel's vision.

The question immediately arises, will the Church be raptured before the twenty-three hundred days begin? We believe so. God has promised that believers will not have to endure His wrath:

I Thessalonians 5:9 For God hath not appointed us to wrath, but to obtain salvation by our Lord Jesus Christ.

Revelation 3:10 Because thou hast kept the word of my patience, I also will keep thee from the hour of temptation, which shall come upon all the world, to try them that dwell upon the earth.

Because the period of 2300 days is one of tribulation, affliction, and suffering world-wide (the "wrath of the lamb"), God will doubtless remove His church from the earth prior to the breaking of the six seals of Revelation 6 and the persecution described in Matthew 24:5-14 which mark the beginning of that ultimate wrath:

Revelation 6:16 And said to the mountains and rocks, Fall on us, and hide us from the face of him that sitteth on the throne, and from the *wrath of the Lamb:*

17 For *the great day of his wrath is come;* and who shall be able to stand?

While we can not know the day or the hour of our Lord's coming, we can discern the signs of the times and Scripture encourages us to do so. Absolutely nothing prevents the Rapture of the Church from occurring at any time. This is in keeping with the doctrine that teaches the imminency of the Lord's return. As for the rest of the world, a major move on the part of Iran to control the Middle East would suggest that the hour is very late indeed. The need to deliver the message of salvation to our friends and neighbors who are unsaved grows more urgent by the hour:

Acts 16:31 And they said, *Believe on the Lord Jesus Christ,* and thou shalt be saved, and thy house.

When the unsaved realize that they must believe, we must tell them *what* they must believe. In I Corinthians 15:1-4 the Apostle Paul made the gospel of the Church Age very clear:

I Corinthians 15:3 For I delivered unto you first of all that which I also received, how *that Christ died for our sins according to the Scriptures;*

4 *And that he was buried, and that he rose again the third day*

according to the Scriptures.

This is the record of God's Son, the gospel which one must believe to receive salvation in this Age of Grace, and the gospel we are constrained by the love of Christ to preach to all the world.

The Church is living even now in a most momentous time. To realize how desperate times are, we need to just consider how quickly the USSR fell, changing the entire world politic almost overnight. The recent war with Iraq was over in 40 days. As we write this, the stage is being set and the players are taking their places for the epilogue of this age. When God's judgment comes, it will be swift and sure.

End Notes

1. Strong, page 85
2. Ibid, page 75
3. Ibid, page 97
4. Ibid, page 81
5. Ibid, page 118
6. Ibid, pages 98
7. Strong, page 102
8. Ibid, page 98
9. BDB, page 31
10. Strong, page 35
11. Ibid, page 63
12. Ibid, page 104
13. HAW, page 809

Epilogue

We recognize that we have challenged an interpretation of Daniel 8 that has for many years been sanctioned as gospel truth by the majority of conservative Christians. Though the world has progressed in finding new truth in other areas, Christianity has by and large been content to accept, with minor reservations, an eschatology first proposed by a pagan, Porphyry (233-305 A.D.), and later amended by Jerome (342-420 A.D.).

Gabriel told Daniel, "Understand, O son of man: for at the time of the end shall be the vision" (Daniel 8:17b). Because believers generally agree that we are living in the last days and because the traditional interpretation of Daniel 8 holds little relevance for our time, we decided that further study of Daniel's vision was needed. Expositors must interpret the Scriptures for their generation, not simply restate the ideas of earlier studies. They must build carefully upon, or else discard, the conclusions of their predecessors. The Apostle Paul warned believers of their responsibility in this regard (emphasis ours):

I Corinthians 3:10   According to the grace of God which is given unto me, as a wise masterbuilder, I have laid the foundation, and another buildeth thereon. *But let every man take heed how he buildeth thereupon.*

Living in a civilization which is running out of time, we must become alert to the signs of our age. The population explosion, with its accompanying problems--starvation, epidemics, and child neglect--deforestation, the contamination of a diminishing water supply, the reckless use of chemicals in our food sources, and the indiscriminate dumping of atomic waste and other lethal materials[1]--these are just a few alarming problems that threaten mankind's existence on the planet placed in our charge.

In these last days God has alerted us not only to the above threats, but also to national movements, many of which are graphically foretold in both Daniel 7 and 8. Regrettably, the traditional interpretation teaches us that this passage largely represents events in the intertestamental period, thus concealing the real meaning of a prophecy which is most relevant to our own day. Our generation is reminiscent of those Christ rebuked at His first advent (emphasis ours):

> Matthew 16:3b O ye hypocrites, ye can discern the face of the sky; *but can ye not discern the signs of the times.*

God has recorded, for our instruction and information, the events that signal an end to this age, but the true account of these times has been obscured by a faulty interpretation of these vital chapters of the book of Daniel.

The Ram, always a symbol of the Medo-Persian Empire (currently known as Iran), is a force with which the world will increasingly have to deal. Iran's influence on OPEC, the oil producing consortium, already causes nervousness in the rest of the world

---

[1] It was recently reported that the former Soviet Union had dumped atomic materials in the ocean in the Arctic Circle. Several atomic submarines with active reactors have been sunk in the area. It was estimated that it would take 50 billion dollars to clean up the dump site.

because of that nation's pressure to raise the price of oil. After remaining obscure to the Western world for centuries, Iran now commands world-wide attention as it arms itself with the latest sophisticated military equipment, including submarines and missiles. Envisioning themselves as the dominant force in the Middle East, in control of the world's main oil supply, and the leader of Islamic Fundamentalism, Iran waits only sufficient time to rebuild their military capability to begin their push "westward, northward, and southward" (Daniel 8:4). The rapid advance of militant Islamic Fundamentalism will doubtless coincide with a disruption of oil distribution, but assuredly when Iran has achieved dominance in the Middle East, it will again provoke the Western nations to defend themselves against another oil embargo.

The Goat, the nations of Javan of the Western world, will at length join forces to do battle with the Ram. But when they have exerted their power and cast the Ram to the earth, the centralized authority of these nations, symbolized by the single horn between the Goat's eyes, will be broken and they will no longer maintain their present influence in the world. From this power vacuum will arise four regional kingdoms, the "four notable ones toward the four winds of heaven" (Daniel 7:2-3; 8:8,22). These four kingdoms were first presented in Daniel 7 as the four beasts out of the sea. They represent the three biblical races of mankind--Shem, Ham, and Japheth--polarized along ethnic lines into kingdoms with Israel, the fourth kingdom, described in Daniel 7:7 as the "beast diverse from them all."

Even now this ethnic polarization is mounting all over the world. Men of different races everywhere are

173

jockeying to gain their share of power, and where borders meet the emotional impact is explosive. The break-up of Yugoslovia and the struggle between Armenia and Azerbaijan are typical of the tensions occurring along both racial and religious lines. These tensions will increase until the borders are defined.

The third ruler of the "diverse beast," the "little horn" will arise quietly and will, by presenting himself as the peace-keeper of the world, quickly be accepted by all ethnic groups. This ruler will initially consolidate his power in the Northern Kingdom of Israel; from there he will incorporate into his kingdom the lion (the Semites), the leopard (the Hamites) and the bear (the Japhethites) as predicted in Revelation 13:2. The "little horn," or Antichrist, will then advance into the Southern kingdom of Israel to conquer and to proclaim himself God of this world.

The signs of the end are all about us. Israel is on the verge of physical division, having been at odds politically, religiously, and culturally for years. The ten horns of the beast described in Daniel 7:7, 20, 24 and in Revelation 13:2, 17:7,12 represent the ten northern tribes of Israel, who will relinguish their authority to the "little horn" for the brief period of his power.

From the time the "little horn" concentrates his attention on the conquest of the Southern Kingdom, only 2300 days (or six years, four months and twenty days) will remain until the Lord Jesus returns. Of those 2300 days, the last 1260 days (or three and one-half years) comprise the "time of Jacob's trouble" when Satan, cast out of heaven, will take personal possession of the "little horn" to accomplish his demonic ends.

While both Daniel 7 and 8 chronicle events setting the stage for the time of the end, the former provides an overview, and the latter a much more detailed portrait of those days. Placing these events in the interval between the testaments and identifying Antiochus Epiphanes, a king of Syria (171-163 B.C.), as the "little horn" seals the book of Daniel to any further understanding of its meaning. Yet such an interpretation admits of too many discrepancies, many of which we have discussed in our previous books. Here we will review the most critical problems with the accepted view on the subject: 1) Porphyry, a pagan philosopher, advanced this interpretation in order to discredit the book of Daniel as prophecy. 2) Jerome, upon whose interpretation the traditional view is based, himself adopted much of Porphyry's intertestamental argument, simply adding Rome as the fourth and final kingdom. 3) Both Porphyry and Jerome used extrabiblical sources (I Maccabees and Josephus) to support their conclusions rather than the biblical text. 4) Internal evidence from exegesis of the text at different points calls into question the traditional interpretation. 5) The ancient Medo-Persian empire was already united when it entered biblical revelation. 6) The Goat must not be identified as Greece at the time of Alexander the Great simply on the basis of the word Grecia, since that word merely refers to Javan. 7) Since the four kingdoms referred to in the visions of both chapters are worldwide in scope, they cannot be limited to those which emerged in the Middle East after the death of Alexander. 8) There are not two "little horns"--a Roman ruler in Daniel 7 and Antiochus Epiphanes in Daniel 8. Such would result in utter confusion, and "God is not the author of confusion" (I Corinthians 14:33). 9) The 2300 days of Daniel 8 did not have their literal fulfillment in the days of Antiochus Epiphanes. Neither did Antiochus stand up against the "Prince of Princes" (Daniel 8:25). Gabriel specifically places this passage "at the time of the end." 10) Antiochus and an unidentified ruler of Russia cannot both be the dreaded "King of the North." Neither can a Pharoah of Egypt and a Roman ruler of the last days both be the "King of the South." The Scriptures do not support such human inventions. 11) Daniel 8 uses 4 different expressions to denote the time of the fulfillment of the vision (verses 17, 19, 23, 26). 12) God's indignation against Israel and the world did not end during the intertestamental period.

A correct exegesis of Daniel 9:24-27 resolves many of these inconsistencies.[2] Biblical scholarship must rethink these positions for our own generation, a generation perishing for want of spiritual truth.

---

[2] See our recent book, *The Seventy Weeks Of Daniel.*

BIBLIOGRAPHY

Abbot-Smith, G. A Manuel, Greek Lexicon of the New Testament, Edinburgh: T & T Clark, 1981.

Chafer, Lewis Sperry, Systematic Theology, 8 Vols. Dallas: Dallas Seminary Press, 1947.

Davidson, A.B., Hebrew Syntax, Edinburgh: T & T Clark, 1894.

Davis, John D., A Dictionary of the Bible, Grand Rapids: Baker Book House, 1984.

Gesenius' Hebrew Grammar, Ed. E. Kautzsch, Revised A.E. Crowley, Oxford: Clarendon Press, 1910.

Harris, Jr., R. Laird, Archer, Gleason L., Waltke, Bruce K., Theological Wordbook of the Old Testament, Chicago: Moody Press, 1980.

Holy Bible, New York: Cambridge University Press, n.d.

Josephus, Flavius. Translated by William Whiston, Peabody: Hendrickson Publishers, 1987.

Keil, Carl Frederich, Delitzsch, Franz, Biblical Commentary of the Old Testament, Trans. James Martin, Grand Rapids: Eerdman, 1945.

Mandela, Nelson, The Struggle is My Life, New York: Pathfinder Press, 1986.

Needham, George C., Prophetic Studies of the International Prophetic Conference, New York: Fleming H. Revell, 1886.

Orr, James, Gen. Ed., The International Standard Bible Encyclopaedia, 5 Vols., Grand Rapids: Eerdman Publishing Company, 1939.

Pentecost, J. Dwight, Things to Come, Grand Rapids: Dunham, 1958.

Scofield, C.I., The Scofield Reference Bible, New York: Oxford, 1917.

Smith, Wilbur M., Introduction to Commentary on Daniel, by Jerome. Grand Rapids: Baker, 1958.

Strong, James, The Exhaustive Concordance of the Bible, New York: Abington Press, 1924.

Talbot, Louis T. The Prophecies of Daniel. Wheaton: Van Kampen, 1954.

Unger, Merrill E., Unger's Bible Handbook, Chicago: Moody Press, 1966.

Walvoord, John F., Daniel, The Key to Prophetic Revelation, Chicago: Moody Press, 1966.

Webster's New World Dictionary of the American Language. New York: The World Publishing Company, 1960.

By

James F. Matheny

and

Marjorie B. Matheny

Is There a Russian Connection?

An Exposition of Ezekiel 37-39
by
James F. Matheny, Th.M.

In his book, Pastor Matheny ably refutes the current popular view that Gog is the prince of Russia and Magog his land and people.

By

James F. Matheny

and

Marjorie B. Matheny

Rethinking the Kingdoms of Daniel 2

Recognizing that the traditional interpretation of the Book of Daniel needed some revision, the authors approached the Kingdoms of Daniel 2 on a word-study basis of the text itself. Some startling truths have emerged from a portion of the Bible long "sealed" to expositors.

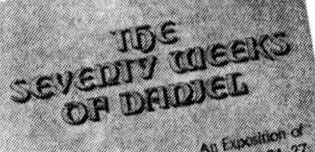

By
James F. Matheny
and
Marjorie B. Matheny

THE SEVENTY WEEKS OF DANIEL

Daniel 9:24-27 is the key to prophecy. These four verses outline the future of the nation of Israel and form the framework for God's plan until the second coming of Christ. The authors considered the text word by word, pointing out some translation errors which are commonly accepted as truth. A chart is included which shows the events of the seventy weeks of years and the text of the book gives a detailed explanation. The corrected translation helps those who would teach the truth of Daniel evaluate their position in light of these new findings.

Order your copy of The Seventy Weeks of Daniel today.

I enclose $6.95 plus $1.25 postage and handling for each copy. Please add sales tax in NC.

Name _____

Address _____

City _____ State _____ Zip _____

Number of copies _____

JAY & ASSOCIATES, PUBLISHERS (704) 885-2062
P.O. Box 2222
Brevard, North Carolina 28712